BRAVER
with Belief

Moving Forward with Hope to Boldly Lead

SHONDA RAMSEY

Braver with Belief
Published by Authentically Created
PO Box 532
Springboro, Ohio 45066
www.authenticallycreated.com

Authentically Created is a division of Lilian Grace Designs, LLC

ISBN 979-8-9898545-4-7 (paperback)
eISBN 979-8-9898545-5-4 (epub)

Library of Congress Control Number: 2025918252

Cover and interior design by Shonda Ramsey

Printed in the United States of America
First Edition 2025

10 9 8 7 6 5 4 3 2 1

091625

Authentically
CREATED

Endorsements

In *Braver with Belief*, author Shonda Ramsey opens up about her own struggles with trusting God and the courage it takes to turn our plans over to Him. I am reminded that He is the only one who can steward our plans well because He is the one who created them. Why do we feel that releasing our plans to Him will disappoint—when in reality it brings joy and success? *Braver with Belief* teaches how to recognize hangups that may be keeping us from fully trusting Him and she walks us through steps to work beyond those hangups to come out on the other side, looking and acting more like Him. And who would want to lead any other way?

—Tami J. Gray, Author of *Fearlessly Unbecoming*

Shonda Ramsey has written another book full of her own personal stories of love, loss, and lessons learned that will encourage and guide you toward a deeper reliance on God as you open your heart to His call into ministry and leadership. Her testimony will show you how healing the vulnerable parts of yourself will enable you to lead others with more confidence and authority through reflective questions and journaling exercises that will help you discover the leader you may have never known was inside you. If you believe God might be calling you into a position of leadership, this book is for you!

—Michelle Bolanger, Author

Braver with Belief is a unique, honest, and truly refreshing approach to walking in your God-given calling through servant leadership.

Shonda beautifully intertwines impactful and relatable glimpses into her own journey with heartfelt and self-reflective moments of faith, inspiring readers to examine their own hearts to become braver with belief and deepen their walk of faith and trust in God.

No matter your capacity in leadership—career, ministry, at home—*Braver with Belief* will meet you where you are and encourage your personal relationship with Jesus as you grow in service of others.

—Niki Banning, Author and StoryGuardian Editor

To Jamie

Thank you for always encouraging me to follow my heart and chase my dreams. You have been my greatest source of inspiration and an exceptional example of a great leader. Your unwavering support and guidance throughout the years has helped me gain the confidence I needed to become a servant leader. I am forever grateful for your friendship and look forward to the many memories that await us.

Contents

Introduction

I used to think something was wrong with me for loving too many things. Too many dreams, too many ideas, too many gifts I didn't know how to use all at once. Over time, I realized there is a term for someone like me: multi-passionate. Even though I loved everything I poured my heart into, I didn't allow myself extra time in my day to work on the things I hoped to. Nevertheless, I was content in my own little world filled with color swatches and paper samples, as I jumped from project to project.

But what happens when you realize you can be a better person and do better things?

One morning, I woke up with an unfamiliar feeling in the pit of my stomach. Nothing earth-shattering had happened that morning. There was no dramatic turning point. But for some reason, I couldn't shake the sense that God was asking me to shift. To change. To release. For the first time in my life, I didn't argue with Him. I simply listened.

God began to work on my heart through stormy weather, showing me areas I needed to release to become the woman He created me to be. I had to undergo a refining process that left me navigating extremely intense emotions, wrestling with the dying of my old self to make way for the new person I was becoming.

Have you ever had the feeling that you need to make a shift in your life—but you didn't know what the shift needed to be? Perhaps you felt a gentle call to step into a new role serving or leading others. Despite knowing you should move towards becoming a servant leader, perhaps you don't feel as though you are qualified or capable to step into such a grandiose role.

That was exactly how I felt. In fact, I would argue with God in His reasoning for calling me to do something I felt I simply couldn't do.

The more I argued with God, the more unhappy I became as I walked in disobedience. I justified my decisions as a means of survival instead of exploring the impossible with God by my side. This refining of my heart that had begun now left a deep pain in its wake as I confronted things I thought I had resolved—but realized I merely buried them deep under the surface.

Knowing God as the ultimate healer, I began the difficult work of mending past hurts so I could better learn self-compassion and diligently work on transitioning my mindset. I longed to be more present each day with my loved ones, friends, and most importantly, with God. Each day would pass me by in a colorful whirlwind of to-do lists and client communications that left me exhausted and unfilled as I crashed into bed each night.

Once I recognized the only way out of the monotony of it all was to stop being afraid and, by making a change, I quickly fell more into pace with God. The only thing He ever wanted is for me to surrender and trust Him. Though that seems simple enough, I found it to be extremely difficult to relinquish control over the situations I found myself in.

Ultimately, I realized what I needed most was to become *braver with belief*. The key to getting there was to deepen my relationship with God in a myriad of ways He revealed to me as I called upon Him more. This process, while not perfect by any means, has prepared and humbled me to confidently step into fulfilling my calling as a servant leader.

Join me, often in real time, as I share with you the difficulties of this shift to becoming all that God created me to be. Even I wasn't prepared for where this shift was about to take me as I watched this book form— as I was writing it. This real-time documentation of my experiences is all new to me. And initially, I fought God on whether to share it in this book. The lesson I learned was that in leading by example, I can best show you how to handle the things life throws at you that may hinder you from fulfilling your calling as a servant leader.

It is my hope and prayer that you find solace and guidance within these pages. You are never alone in your struggles. There are often others facing things that cause them to doubt or stumble, too. The way I've been able to work through them has been extremely helpful for me. It undoubtedly could help you too.

Faith in the Fire

I wrote this book as a spiritual refinement. I encourage you to take your time in each chapter, completing all the steps at the end before you advance in the book. One chapter may take you an hour or a year; the choice is yours to make. But it is important to not skip through chapters, or you may miss an important step that could alter your outcome.

Each chapter offers a valuable life lesson, giving you the chance to get to know me and the process of refining my heart to be better prepared for servant leadership. It is in these life lessons I share my most vulnerable states, some of which I have never shared with anyone before.

As I share my struggles through completely shifting the direction I am taking in business, ministry, and lifestyle, you'll see me not just as a guide, but as a fellow traveler in this shift. By sharing my own vulnerabilities, I hope to bridge the gap between us, making this more than just words on a page. It's my sincerest wish that as you turn these pages, you feel a sense of companionship, knowing you're not navigating this season alone. Consider me not just an author but a friend in your corner, rooting for you every step of the way.

What You Can Expect at the End of Each Chapter

The Unseen Truth - The thing that is often difficult to unearth from the hiding place we've put it in. I leave you with a question to get you thinking about your life and how my life lesson can be applied. I encourage you to write it in your journal and add your response to the question when you feel ready.

Braver with Belief - Where we can find scripture to support our desire to become braver in His Word and apply it to our lives. I share verses from the Bible that helped me work through my valuable life lesson, and show you what actions we can take where bravery is found.

The Strength in Letting Go - What this means in our current moment. I take my valuable life lesson and teach you how to navigate similar situations. I encourage you to consider one thing you can let go of to become braver with belief.

Moving Forward with Hope - How taking action can propel you forward with the hope that you are closer to becoming a servant leader. When you first start reading, fear of becoming a leader may override the hope of the goodness leading will bring. When I was in the storm, there was no hope visible. But with action, hope became evident.

Braver Choices - Actionable steps you can take to become braver with belief as you step into the role of servant leader. I have broken it down for you in a way that is easier to remember: **B.R.A.V.E.R.**

Brighten: An action taking call to service to refine our hearts as we discover the area in which to serve.

Reflect: A prayer that covers the emotions felt within each chapter with a promise to let go of the things we need to, so we can keep moving forward.

Act: An action taking exercise that forces us to get up and move forward.

Verse: Memorization of a Bible verse that helps us remember the lesson within the chapter.

Explore: An action taking exercise to help us explore new possibilities we may not have yet thought of.

Renew: A journal prompt for us to reflect with God in solitude.

The exercises may be physical activities I instruct you to do, or they could be journal prompts to spend time in solitude with God. These actionable steps have been thoughtfully curated to help you do the work needed to prepare your heart to begin to lead with a servant heart.

Resources to Have on Hand

This book is an interactive book, with encouragement to act on refining your heart and preparing to lead. There are resources listed here that I personally use daily and will help you maximize your experience. I recommend you gather as many of these items as possible and put them in a tote bag or some other small mobile container so you can take them with you wherever you choose to do the activities mentioned in this book. I call this my Growth Bag.

Growth Bag Contents:

- *Braver with Belief* Book
- *Called to Serve* Guided Journal
- Pocket or digital Bible
  - YouVersion App (or other similar)
- Journal
- Pens
- Paper (loose)
- Colored pencils, markers, or crayons
- Mirror
- Sticky notes or a dry erase marker
- Spotify Playlist

A Curated Spotify Playlist that coordinates with *Braver with Belief*

A glimpse into the *Called to Serve* **Guided Journal**

All that stands between you and becoming braver with belief is an open heart and mind. I ask that you give yourself grace and patience as you work through some difficult exercises to get to the root of what God is asking you to let go of as you prepare your heart for becoming a servant leader.

Friend, I know this feels scary. You may be afraid and feel alone in your desire to answer the calling God has placed on your heart to become a leader. I know this because I am right there beside you. You aren't alone; God wants you to know He has prepared and equipped you for a time such as this. You have what it takes to be a leader. You just need to refine your heart a bit to help you confidently lead

I hope that by sharing with you my innermost thoughts and fears, you will come to know and understand that while I may not be able to fully understand your experiences and expertise, I can empathize. Will you join me as we boldly step out in faith and with a resounding yes, fulfill the calling God has placed on our hearts?

Dedication

I, _____, commit to not only reading "Braver With Belief," but also promise to open my heart as I engage with and apply the journal prompts and exercises provided at the end of each chapter as I begin to refine my heart and confidently step into the role of servant leadership.

Signed,   Date:_____

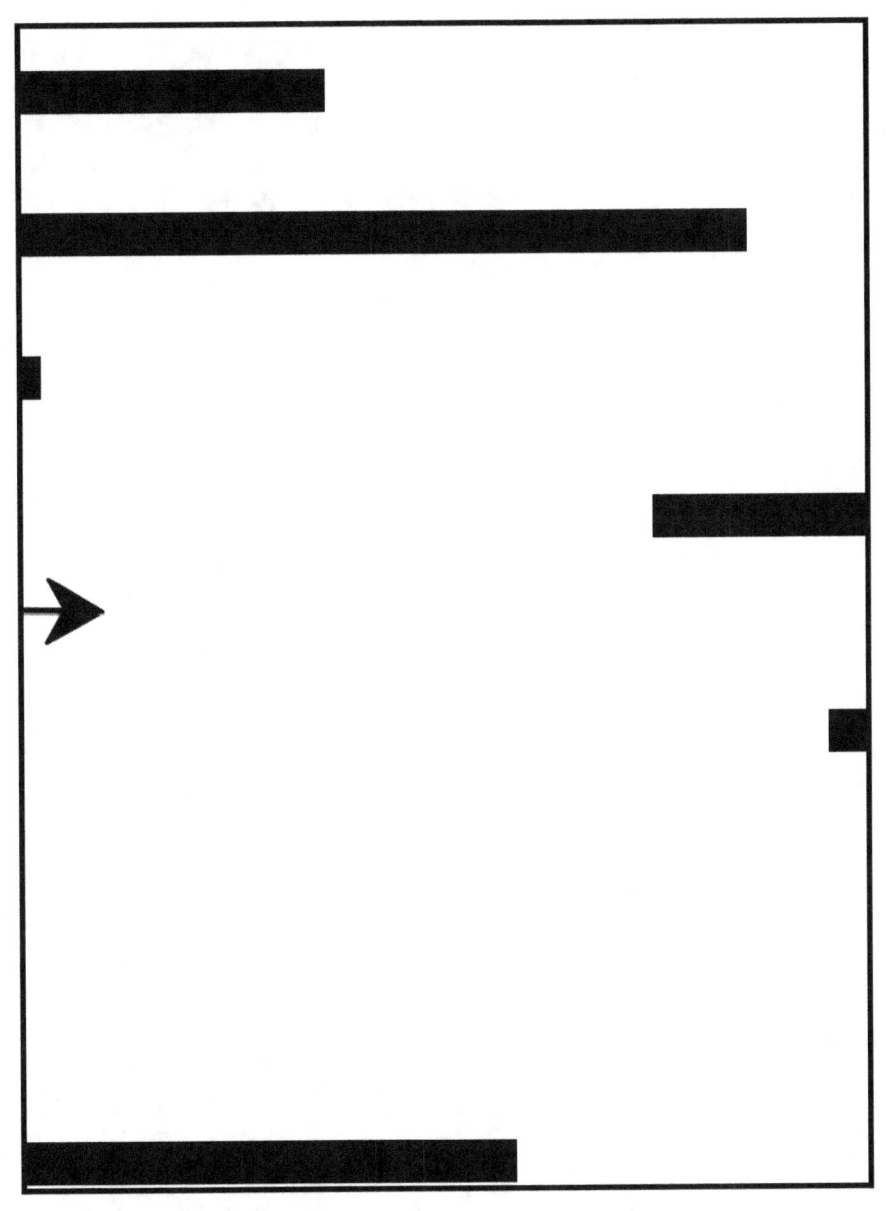

chapter one

Unexpected Circumstances

After working incredibly hard to figure out who I am authentically, I settled into monotonous habits. Each day resembled a cozy space that felt like a warm blanket wrapped around me on a chilly winter night. The inviting soft glow of candlelight kept me fixated comfortably in place, never wanting to leave. Comfort slowed my pace—which wasn't a bad thing—at first. Everything I did was at a natural rhythm as each day moved forward. Yet something still felt off.

Perhaps it was a little too comfortable and familiar as I settled into that cozy place. Though I enjoyed every moment life offered, I regretted not prioritizing my calling to be a leader during the long winter months as I moved more slowly. Time had passed while I remained unchanged and unwilling to bravely step out in faith.

Spring was finally here, which meant RV season was upon us in full swing. I was eager to get away to a place where I could spend time in nature as I sought direction for what would be my next new beginning.

Doubt filled my mind as I questioned whether now was the time to focus on my calling, or if perhaps continuing forward at this comfortable pace was the right thing for me. My thoughts contradicted themselves and created a perfect storm within me. Paralyzed in place due to fear of moving forward with ideas, I relied on the opinions of peers—which only contributed to my inability to make a decision. I recognized old patterns emerging as I reminded myself to be brave so I could move forward. *But how…*

May 2024 | A Trip I'll Never Forget

Excitement filled the cab of the truck as Mike and I crossed over the bridge on our way out of Ohio and into Kentucky with the RV in tow. Music played our favorite road trip playlist, and we loudly sang along as we moved farther away from home on our way to a campsite we had never been to before. The website promised us lakeside views and boat rentals for lake exploration, which only added to our growing excitement as we made plans for the weekend.

As we continued southwest, I joked with Mike about how we never get the timing right when planning a trip; we always forget to account for the fact we are towing the RV, which slows us down. The drive in took far longer than we initially thought it would, and we wondered if we made a big mistake in picking this location when we had to take narrow country roads quite a distance from the interstate.

The campground was not what we expected when we arrived. We followed our camp guide down extremely narrow roads with little room for maneuvering. It was hectic as we dodged trucks with boats, children on bikes, adults on golf carts, and people randomly standing in the middle of the road. It was a stark difference compared to our preferred more laid back campgrounds with scenic views and fewer people.

Mike and I arrived at our campsite, and after some maneuvering to level the RV, we had everything set up to enjoy the evening to the fullest. Despite our choice of a lakeside spot, the campsite in front of us partially obstructed our view. We were both disappointed that the premium price we paid for the views didn't deliver its promised feature. Instead, we stared at the RV directly in front of us, blocking most of the lake. This was our first trip to Kentucky in our RV—and I was fairly certain it would be the last trip to this location.

Trying not to let the campsite completely sour our mood and ruin our anniversary trip, we sat outside to enjoy the sunset. The sun began to set over the lake, and it cast a warm glow of orange over everything it touched. I took a few photographs and videos, telling Mike how grateful I was for the ten times zoom feature on my phone camera which allowed me to get around the RV in front of us to see a small sliver of lake. We sat outside for as long as we could stand the cicadas dive-bombing us—and spent time removing them from our Yorkie, Coco's mouth when she would inevitably catch them as they flew by.

Once safely back inside, we enjoyed some time together watching one of our favorite shows. The long drive in had completely worn us both out and we struggled to stay awake. Before going to sleep that night, I checked the weather for the next day and discovered some potentially bad weather could be in the area. If the app was correct, we could not rent a boat after all, which further added to our disappointment. As a precautionary measure, we plugged in our weather radio and tuned it to the nearest county before settling in for the night.

Upon waking the next morning, I checked the weather forecast again and mentioned to Mike that we may need to keep monitoring it. No sooner had I said those words, I received a text from my parents telling me a tornado had touched down a few counties over from where we were. The news showed it was a slower moving cell of storms, which gave us a little time to determine what to do next.

Because there was no way I wanted to be stuck in a tornado shelter with strangers while not feeling clean, I quickly showered. As I reached to turn the water off, the skylight overhead turned green. I knew we were in trouble. I rushed out of the shower and quickly got dressed, shouting at Mike to get Coco ready to head for safety.

Mike wasn't sure what to make of me in my frenzied state, but I had this feeling that we needed to get out and we needed to get out fast. As I rushed to put on socks and shoes, our phones alerted us we were now in a tornado warning zone and we needed to seek shelter immediately. Out to the truck we went, dodging rain, as Mike secured Coco in the back. We both jumped in the front to ride it out, still unsure if there was an actual threat in our vicinity as we looked around at what the other campers were doing.

The wind and rain picked up, and I pleaded with Mike to drive us to the bathhouse shelters that were located just behind our campsite. We rushed out of the truck into the pouring rain to the first side of the shelter, only to discover it was completely full. Drenched, we ran to the other side, where graciously, a whole family moved into one stall to make room for us to squeeze in with them.

Despite feeling a sense of gratitude for their willingness to make room for us, I had an uneasy energy that welled up inside of me. This feeling of uncertainty felt heavy in my heart as Mike stepped back into the corner with Coco in his arms and I took my place in front of them both to shield her in between us.

In our rush, I had forgotten to grab Coco's leash from the truck. We had to hold her, which was extremely difficult because of the space constraints and her weight. Mike sat her down on the ground between our legs to shelter her from other dogs that were also in there. Although she stood shaking and visibly scared, she was surprisingly quiet.

The wind speed picked up. I looked up out of the window above my head and watched as a tree bent sideways, just as there was a loud clap of thunder and the lights went out. Fear gripped my heart tightly. On instinct, I stepped closer to Mike and laid my head on his shoulder while simultaneously reaching down to comfort Coco. My heart pounded so loudly, I was certain the people next to me could hear it.

Road Closed Ahead

Others around us were just as unsettled as we were. In that moment, all I could do was cling to Mike and Coco and pray that God would keep us safe and help us get out of there alive. There was nothing more I could do. I was in an unexpected circumstance that I had absolutely no control over.

I have heard it said when you find yourself in a situation like this, your life flashes before your eyes. While my life didn't flash before my eyes, I suddenly regretted not expressing my love and gratitude to Mike that morning or calling my parents to hear their voices instead of just texting. With my head bowed, I pleaded with God to keep us all safe and promised to do better and to be a better person. I confessed my apologies to Him for being disobedient in avoiding my calling, and vowed if we survived this storm, I would begin the steps needed to lead. Eventually, the wind died down, and the rain slowed into a light shower. I was relieved and grateful we survived. I realized that nothing makes you more humble than huddling in a wet campground bathhouse with strangers for a half an hour as Mother Nature is wreaking havoc all around you.

In our time spent in the shelter, we found out that two more storms were coming right behind this one, each growing in severity and intensity. We couldn't risk staying in the RV during another tornado. There was an unspoken knowing between Mike and I that this situation was bad—and we needed to safely and quickly get out. The campground hosts who were huddled with us in the restrooms gave us the all clear to head back out. In silence, we made our way to the truck, stepping over large branches and debris along the way.

As we drove back to our campsite, damage was everywhere. Fallen branches covered other RVs, trees blocked the roadways, and the wind scattered dented trash cans everywhere. My heart pounded loudly, and I held my breath as we turned the corner to our spot, unsure of what state we'd find our RV in.

Our RV had a near-miss as the tree in between us and the site next to us fell on top of their RV and directly behind ours. I exhaled as Mike and I assessed the RV and took photographs and videos just in case we would need them. We packed up our belongings so we could get out as quickly as possible.

I don't know what we expected to find once we pulled out of the campsite, but our reality was a genuine nightmare. Trees blocked all roads out of the campsite except for one, but that was a one-way entrance. With the help of staff, we had to drive to the back of the campground, do a loop around, and come back past our campsite before we could get to the main road leading into the area we were in.

Because many others were also trying to get out, the campground was pure chaos. In one area, other vehicles pushed us off the road. I grabbed hold of the door handle tightly as we almost got stuck in a deep ditch. Another near miss! I wasn't sure if I could handle any more stress without completely letting the floodgate of emotions open wide—but I knew I needed to keep it together to help get us out of there.

An hour later, we reached the main driveway in and out of the campground. We couldn't believe our eyes. Uprooted trees in the power lines lay suspended sideways mere feet from several tents. We were silent as we slowly drove past, neither of us sure of what to say. We eventually made it back to the main road. However, what we found was more of the same.

Trees were down, blocking parts of the road. Once we finally got around them, we found the road we needed was closed. Cell towers were down, which created spotty signals for our GPS as I tried repeatedly to find an alternate route to the interstate. In a car, it wouldn't be as much of an issue to take a detour, but when you are in a large truck pulling an RV trailer behind you, there are some roads you simply cannot take.

We pushed forward as we tried to make our way back to the highway and begin our trek back home, a five-hour journey. The damage we saw on the way home that day is something that will stick with me forever. It went on for miles. As I wiped away the tears that eventually fell from my eyes, I breathed a prayer of gratitude for God's goodness in keeping us safe.

The farther we drove, the more time had passed, which allowed for the second storm cell to catch up with us. The rain grew heavier with each new mile. It was extremely difficult to navigate because of wind gusts, low visibility—and our fuel level had become uncomfortably low. We came to an exit with diesel on the gas sign and pulled off to fill up the tank just as another large storm hit. We found ourselves in the middle of a heavy downpour as the wind rocked us back and forth despite being under the awning at the station. On pure adrenaline, Mike filled the tank as I ran inside to use the restroom and pick up a much-needed cup of coffee for him.

God Answered My Prayers

Mike and I found it difficult to keep up to date with the ever-changing weather situation since our signal was weak much of the time. I was so grateful for my parents during our trip home. They were our eyes and ears the whole eight hours. Once we were home safe, exhausted by the emotional toil the day had on both of us, we collapsed on the couch and talked through all that we were both feeling.

This experience caused us to question if we wanted to continue to RV—or if it was time to cut our losses and move on. We talked about the things we loved while camping and the troubles we faced with the changing weather patterns and unknown and potentially dangerous situations that could arise. We used to have a dream of taking the RV all around the USA to visit all the states and go places we had not yet visited. What we learned early on, however, was while this was good in theory, it wasn't workable for our lifestyle and careers.

The unpredictability of things like the weather and wear and tear on both the truck and RV created an additional problem we didn't fully consider when we were just starting out camping locally. This wasn't our first trip far from home, but we deemed it our last trip at that distance. We wanted to ensure if we ever found ourselves in a similar situation, it would be much easier and quicker to get home.

You may feel that decision was a drastic shift for us to make, and in that moment, I would have likely argued that it was the correct decision. However, now that time has passed and the emotions from the day are not as intense, we have discussed what we could do to be better prepared for situations like this while camping. Because we love camping so much, we both need frequent trips to nature to recharge, making it impossible to give up.

From our last experience, we realized a weather radio provided us with only the bare essentials for severe weather alerts. However, Mike and I lacked much beyond that, so we are now discussing preparations for spring camping. We don't want to fear something we enjoy doing, but we want to be weather alert while camping—and having a contingency plan in place to either cancel or postpone the trip is also important.

During the storm, God answered my prayers and kept us safe, but I couldn't help but wonder what lesson He had for me through this experience. Looking back, I realize I was still clinging tightly to controlling my life and not allowing God the chance to lead.

Shortly after the tornado experience, my book, *Authentically Anchored*, was scheduled to be published. Though I had anchored myself in Christ, I still had more work to do to prepare my heart to be a leader.

When I think about the similarities in this situation and my life, I can see how being prepared is beneficial. Often, I get wrapped up in my schedule and become easily distracted. It can become overwhelming as I try to do many things at once, all on my own. Days could go by where I am so focused on the tasks I have set for myself, I forget to slow down and ask God for direction or shelter.

Instead of hoping for the best, I prefer to be in control of my destiny. Despite my efforts to be decisive on impulse, the idea fills me with anxiety. Organization and preparation create predictability and bring me happiness and a stronger sense of self. This character trait felt like a giant flaw in my personality. Seeking strength and wisdom, I became more aware of my response to unexpected circumstances.

The added stress, I realized, would trigger a wave of panic as I tried to adapt to fit the sudden change of plans. It seemed to be worse on the days I felt more stressed and tired from lack of good sleep the night before. This would create that perfect storm within me, taking my expectation coupled with the sudden change and turning it into stress as it fed the entire system until I felt like my insides were swirling around at rapid speed.

Ultimately, this out-of-control feeling would create a reaction rather than a response, which became problematic. Through conviction from the Holy Spirit, I began recognizing the uncontrolled behavior I had within my reaction. This made me extremely remorseful for becoming a person whose emotions controlled the way I reacted to others, instead of responding in love.

I had a strong desire to be someone who always led with love; however, my reality was far from that. I was creating situations in my life that had caused me to stumble and remove myself from God time and time again as I tried to fix it myself. The desire to change was strong, however, I was still trying to control every aspect around being different.

Eventually, I realized I was getting nowhere on my own. My time spent in prayer shifted to include more time in silence, allowing God the chance to show me what He wanted me to do in certain situations. This began preparing my heart to loosen the hard edges that had formed over the years, as it showed me the areas I needed improvement.

I challenged myself to invite God to join me as I tried to figure out a problem, or when I would become stressed over plans that changed suddenly. During my prayer time, I prayed for patience and self-control, realizing these were two areas in which I was lacking—and contributing to my stress. Over time, I stopped putting expectations on people, and I also came up with a contingency plan in case of a scheduling shift that might occur.

Be Patient with Yourself

The changes I chose to implement appeal to the parts of me that thrive in an organized and controlled environment, while still allowing room for adaptability. By choosing new habits to focus on that I knew would work with me, instead of against me, I was establishing a situation that would help me be successful in my efforts. I knew success would create a desire to continue in the same direction.

Unexpected circumstances will always come, even if everything is going exactly how you'd like it to be going. Because you cannot control the unexpected, the next best thing you can control is your response to them. This can be tricky, especially if you naturally are a reactive person and have a difficult time taming powerful emotions.

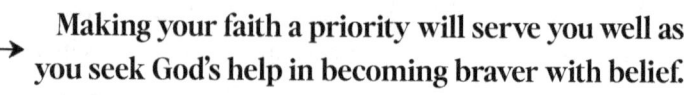 **Making your faith a priority will serve you well as you seek God's help in becoming braver with belief.**

The more you lean into your faith, the more you are allowing room for a transformation to occur as you shift into becoming the person God is lovingly guiding you to be. Avoid becoming complacent with your faith when you don't see or feel an immediate change. Habits take a long time to form. I realize my negative habits result from long-term exposure to the same behavior without correction. To redirect your actions is also similar to retraining yourself or starting over again. Be patient with yourself. And on days when you feel like giving up, may I encourage prayer and an invitation for God's help instead?

Know too, as you age, it becomes more difficult to both identify areas needed for improvement and course-correct the behaviors you've grown accustomed to. I say this as lovingly as possible, and as someone who understands the middle-aged struggle that occurs after forty. We are tired, we don't have extra time, and we aren't playing games. Maybe that is the Gen-X in me, but know you aren't alone in these thoughts and feelings. Also know it's not too late to change. Remember, you can do hard things if you choose to do them.

This brings me to my last point. Choose to make your faith a daily priority. If you desire a closer relationship with God, the only way you'll achieve that is by inviting Him into conversation each day. I'm not talking about the half-awake-as-you're-falling-asleep prayer because you forgot-to-pray-earlier kind of conversation. When something happens that causes you to stop in your tracks and wrestle with the urge to scream, this would be an excellent time to slow down and invite God into a conversation about the situation. Tell Him how mad you are. He already knows, but He still wants to hear it from you.

Strengthening your faith is a multi-step process that involves prayer, petition, study, and putting all you have learned into practice. The more often you do these things together, the stronger your faith will continue to grow. I choose to do these things because I desire to be a better person for my family, my friends, and strangers I have yet to meet. I recognized my negativity was a problem that kept me from being able to connect with others more naturally as I would keep them at arm's length.

If you desire to be there for those who need you, you can be much more prepared for this by first getting out of the cozy space you've settled in and begin making time to strengthen your foundation. By building your foundation in faith, you'll be far more prepared to withstand the storms that are undoubtedly coming your way.

The Unseen Truth

It's easier to believe what you can see than it is to accept the truth of what you do not know. If I go back in time to the first day we arrived at the campground, I see that my attitude was one showing I was not open to new experiences in a strange place. I defaulted to complaining about the lack of views, the overcrowded campground, and the millions of cicadas buzzing about. These were all the things I could see and hear all around me. In my negative mindset, I dreaded the remainder of the trip before it even started.

Instead of getting to know my campground neighbors, I hid inside the RV, away from everything that annoyed me. After the tornado, I spoke with our neighbor, whose RV had a tree across the top. And I discovered that while the tornado was coming through, he and his family were attending the local church. His peaceful demeanor stayed with me as I questioned why I felt so anxious while he did not.

Is it possible that I had taken my eyes off of Jesus, which was contributing to my panic? Because the enemy uses fear, distracting us from fully trusting God, I believe that my survey of my surroundings filled me with an overwhelming sense of fear. My palms grew sweaty, my heart rate increased, and I struggled to breathe as I fixated on what could have happened to us instead of appreciating being spared those alternative outcomes.

When you can clearly see destruction all around you, there's no denying what you just went through was awful. Could it have been worse? Absolutely, but in that moment, you don't realize that in all of it, God was right beside you because you didn't see Him visually. The way to be certain of His presence is to pay attention to your thoughts and feelings during moments like this. Once you become more in-tune with your needs, your body, and your emotions, it will become easier to see and feel the Holy Spirit all around you.

What storms in your life caused you to take your eyes off of Jesus and question whether or not God was with you through it?

Braver with Belief

"For our light and momentary troubles are achieving for us an eternal glory that far outweighs them all. So we fix our eyes not on what is seen, but on what is unseen, since what is seen is temporary, but what is unseen is eternal."

2 Corinthians 4:17-18

In order to become braver with belief, we must first squash the fear of the unseen and unknown. I recognize that fear is often the driving factor in my response to heightened situations. Because I am a person who prefers to control situations, I have had to remind myself this is incorrect thinking, and God needs to be in control.

While I could not see what God was doing in the unexpected circumstances I found myself in, I could feel Him working with me when I cried for His help. The realization of His presence the entire time didn't come to me when I was facing the storm, but months after, when I had time to work through and process the emotional toll it had taken on me.

Let me remind you that though you cannot see God, He is still right there beside you. Your present storm is temporary and insignificant compared to what awaits you eternally. I know the storm feels heavy and permanent, but with time, you'll soon realize the importance of the lesson within that frightening moment. Redirect your attention and priorities away from what is in this physical world to focus on what God has waiting for you.

The Strength in Letting Go

Recurring dreams of being in the middle of a tornado have become all too familiar to me. I rush to the basement for safety, only to find myself in a room made entirely of windows as the tornado inches closer. Right as the tornado hits the building I'm in, I always wake up. Each time, the dream is slightly different. But they all end the same: with me waking in the dark, breathless and terrified, my heart ferociously pounding.

Life sometimes feels like these dreams, as my world swirls all around me and I desperately try to grab everything I can save at once. As I collect moments and things, I find I cannot save it all as I watch it being swept up into the funnel and dispersed farther away from me.

I stand in the aftermath and wonder where I went wrong, as a gentle whisper reminds me I took my eyes off of Jesus. I turn to face Him, tears in my eyes, as He smiles softly and says, "Shonda, I'm always here, I can help you, all you have to do is ask."

Nothing swept away matters. And that realization changed me. My hopes and dreams were things I set for myself without first asking God if that was what He had in mind for me. My plans and preparations were for things that I was prideful about, not for things God instructed me to do. I can repurpose the rubble now lying near me into beautiful building blocks to become the woman God guides me to be, and He will do the same for you, once you release your need to control your situation.

Does life feel like everything you ever wanted is just out of reach? I have felt that way for as long as I can remember. I want to encourage you to take some time to consider if those hopes and dreams outside your reach are your vision, or if they are God's. Maybe what you need right now is to let go of everything you are controlling, to be swept up in the proverbial tornado, to be tossed away from you as you turn to Jesus and ask for His help in rebuilding.

Moving Forward with Hope

Most unexpected circumstances are beyond our control, which can induce fear and anxiety as we struggle to regain a sense of control in the situation. Our insistent need to be in charge of our own outcomes drives us to cling a bit too tightly to most situations. Letting go of the desire to control these situations and allow your faith to override your fear will restore your hope. We also hold on to grudges longer than we should, and in the next chapter, we'll talk about how letting go of grudges will help you become even braver with faith.

Braver Choices

Actionable steps you can take to become braver with belief as you step into the role of servant leader. I have broken it down for you in a way that is easier to remember: **B.R.A.V.E.R.**

Brighten: An action taking call to service to refine our hearts as we discover the area in which to serve.

Serving Others: Reach out to a friend who is facing a storm right now. Give your friend the space needed to express their feelings. Offer support any way you feel led.

Reflect: A prayer that covers the emotions felt within each chapter with a promise to let go of the things we need to, so we can keep moving forward.

> *Father, I am so sorry that I took my eyes off of you. Help me release my constant need to control everything I do and allow you the chance to lead me where you want. Please forgive me for focusing on the things that I can see and not trusting your guidance. Amen.*

Act: An action taking exercise that forces us to get up and move forward.

Spend time in solitude. Close your eyes and focus on the storm you are currently facing in your life. Cry out to Jesus, and lay it all at His feet.

Verse: Memorization of a Bible verse that helps us remember the lesson within the chapter.

Write the following scripture and post it somewhere you'll see it every day; maybe a bathroom mirror, refrigerator, or your home office. Memorize it and refer to it when you feel alone in the midst of the storm.

> *"Cast all your anxiety on him because he cares for you."*
>
> 1 Peter 5:7

Explore: An action taking exercise to help us explore new possibilities we may not have yet thought of.

Doodle Exercise: Draw a tornado in the middle of a piece of paper. Draw images or write words coming from all angles of the tornado that reflect the storms you are currently facing. Add in anything you are clinging too tightly onto control. Destroy it when finished and release it all by offering it up in prayer to God.

Renew: A journal prompt for us to reflect with God in solitude.

Journal Prompt: Though I cannot see God, I lay these storms at His feet.

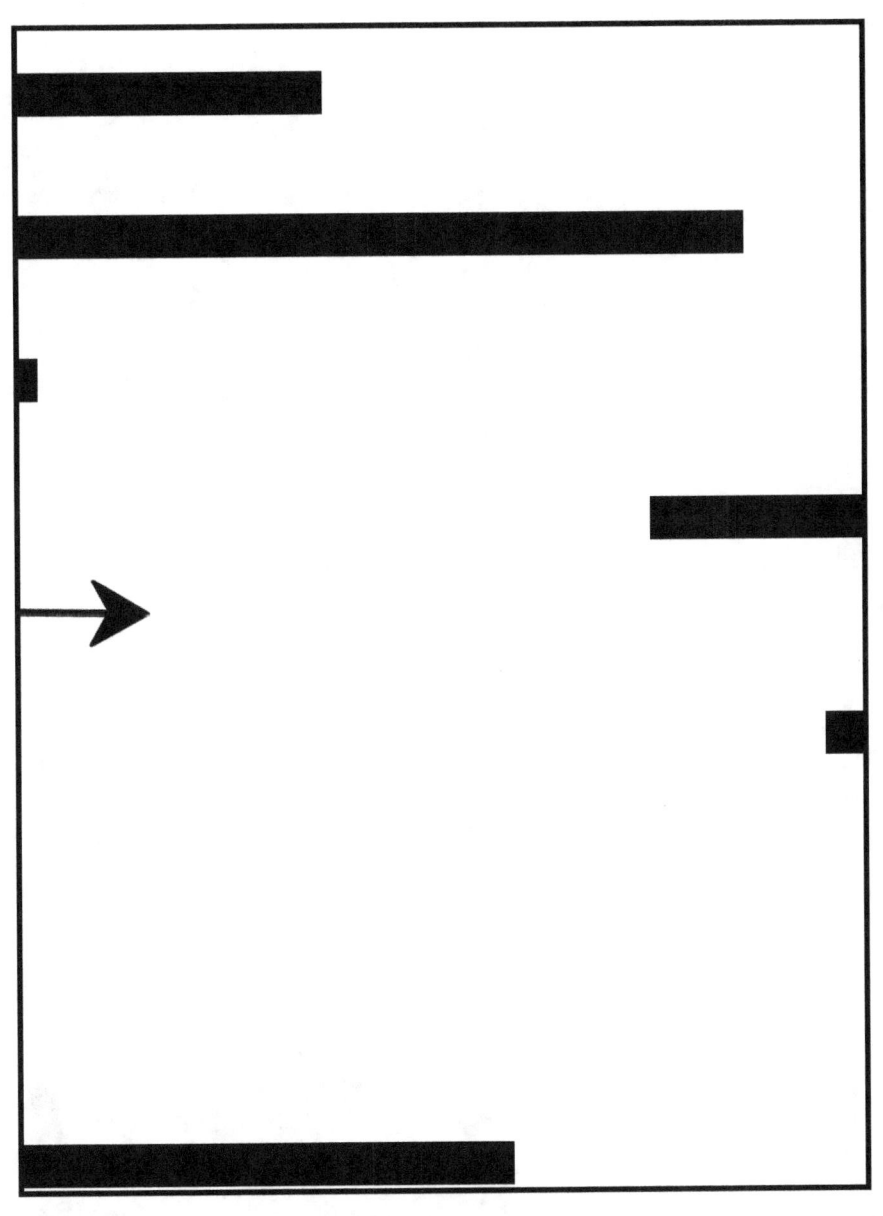

chapter Two

Letting Go of Grudges

Surviving the storm put things into perspective, but also dredged up past hurts I hadn't fully released. I struggled with negative thoughts that would creep back in when I was most vulnerable.

The one thing I wanted most in this world was to be a mother. Unfortunately, despite this being one of my biggest desires, it simply wasn't possible for me. Not being able to fulfill my longing, I struggled to fully cope with the loss of my greatest dream. This constant reminder of what others had perceived to be a major handicap is the very thing I allowed to become the excuse for not making progress.

Everywhere I went, there were smiling women surrounded by their energetic children. Instead of being filled with joy at the sight, I felt deep remorse. I had developed this idea that being infertile meant I was incomplete, and there was no way God would call an incomplete woman to serve.

What could a woman like me teach others? I wrestled with this question day after day as my warm blanket beckoned me from my chair. As I sat comfortably in its warmth, I laughed at the preposterous thought that God could, in fact, use me to help others. Though I felt called to teach women, I believed I could only teach about motherhood—something I never fully experienced. It never occurred to me that perhaps there was something else I could teach—that motherhood wasn't the only subject. Once I let go of the expectation of having a life where I could teach about motherhood, only then could I move forward.

It became easier and easier to sit idly by as each day passed without fulfilling the calling placed upon my heart. Bravery was a word that had not yet found its way into my vocabulary, and most certainly was not a term I would use to describe who I was. I did, however, envy others who were not only brave, but had confidence felt by all those they touched.

A Childless Woman

These days, jealousy seems to be an emotional response that tends to be the default more often than not. While scrolling social media, it is easy to become jealous of what others possess, how successful they appear, or even how beautiful they may look. We compare our shortcomings to their fruitfulness and become frustrated with how everyone but us is being awarded the finer things in life.

If you allow comparison to go unchecked for too long, you risk being discontent in the beautiful life you have. It's hard to think that someone out there may, in fact, be looking at you in the same manner that you are looking at someone else. There is always going to be someone who wishes for the things you have in life that are missing from theirs.

Jealousy is something I struggled with for a very long time. When I first discovered I was infertile because of polycystic ovarian syndrome, I struggled with accepting that I may never be a mom in the traditional sense. Repeatedly, I watched as there were pregnancy announcements from the masses, including those who clearly didn't want the precious gift they carried inside of them. The thought that a loving God could so obviously pass me over for motherhood while giving it to countless other women was a painful struggle.

My desire to be a mother began in my youth and only grew stronger. For a long time, I felt incomplete because I couldn't fulfill this inner desire. It was exceptionally difficult for me to cope with the cruelty of being infertile in a world focused not only on women having babies, but knowing our worth somehow is also tied in with it.

Infertility can completely break you. You feel your womanhood is taken away despite trying everything you can to fulfill this one deep desire you've had since you were young. Society tends to label women without children as broken. To make matters worse, they treat you in such a manner as they look at you with pity in their eyes when they discover your truth.

Judgment comes in many forms when people hear you don't have children. I feel as a society, we've made it acceptable to ask the potentially intrusive question "Do you have children?" even when first meeting a stranger. These awkward encounters usually would leave me frustrated as the person asking began to stammer and ask more questions that only further exacerbated the frustration. So many times I wanted to shout, "No, it's not that I don't want to have children; it's that I cannot have them."

I hated that I had to constantly overshare complex details of my very personal situation when questions would continue to come. Sure, I could have simply stated it was none of their business. But you see, that isn't who I am. I felt I owed an explanation to make them more comfortable around a hurting woman. However, the nurturing and compassionate side in me put their feelings above my own.

The questions didn't stop there, and I would usually find myself in another precarious position as my uncomfortableness became increasingly so with each new question. Questions like: "How do you spend all the free time you have without kids in the house?" And "How much money are you saving by not spending it on school or sporting fees for kids?" I listened to the complaints of their children sucking their lives from them day in and day out when all they wanted was to use the restroom alone.

I would leave the conversation, shaking my head in disbelief that they would complain to me about having the very thing I wanted more than anything. The lack of compassion and empathy towards my situation felt abundantly clear. It was interactions like these that made me feel like I couldn't share how I was feeling or coping with my infertility struggles. They simply wouldn't understand.

As a childless woman, I have had to work extremely hard for everything I have accomplished, and still I feel it's not enough. Something seems to be missing. The grief I carry from not having children often makes going through each day extremely difficult. Grief shows up unexpectedly, stopping any thoughts of fully functioning. There have been countless days where the mere act of getting out of bed was excruciating. I have spent extra time in the shower to hide the fact that my grief was so heavy; I couldn't stop crying as the hot water poured on top of me.

If I made it to my office to do work by eight in the morning, that meant I'd already conquered the desire to wallow in self-pity—a monumental feat most days. I have found once I am in my office, I can usually stick to the plan I have in place for the day. It helps that I love the work I do. Still, I have often defaulted to allowing my work to replace downtime, in which I process emotions as a means to avoid the very emotions I have.

After spending the day fulfilling everything mapped out in my planner and checking off the to-do lists, I dread the sudden shift from being in motion to becoming motionless. That's the thing with grief; you can tame the way it causes you to feel by distracting it with busyness. Once you stop being busy, you must confront the feelings that emerge. It is in this space I had to confront grief head-on to understand why I allow it to hold power over me. What I learned was that grief is something that remains a part of me. By giving myself grace in this area, I have been able to learn new ways of coping with it.

While families are enjoying evenings with their children, I sit in an empty home, often confronted by my own thoughts. Instead of settling into another night of binge-watching streaming channels, I may choose to pick up my laptop, put on some jazz, and write. Other times, I may study a new skill or practice drawing digitally to enhance my graphic design portfolio. The mere act of doing something worthwhile with my time is enough to trigger a mindset shift that carries through to the next day. Now when I wake up, rather than struggling, I am excited to do it all over again.

Identifying Grudges

Not everyone can live their lives the way I choose to live mine. I was fortunate to transition from a full-time job to a full-time business. I went from working for someone else to working for myself. My tireless efforts to sustain my business match my passion for my work.

When we fostered children, I had to leave my career to care for the children's needs full-time because of the sheer number of appointments we had. A career was the last thing on my mind as I faced the demands of caring for two children with needs greater than my own, while also navigating the role of motherhood overnight.

Then the children left, and I re-entered the workforce, where I remained for quite some time before starting my business. Starting my business was met with severe criticism, skepticism, and judgment. For eight years, I struggled mentally with the backlash I received from others that stemmed from my career choice and their lack of understanding. The awkward conversations about infertility were now replaced by accusations that being a business owner instead of working at a corporation meant I was lazy.

Instead of celebrating my accomplishments, I retreated inward to avoid these discussions and the pain they brought. Again, I shrunk down who I was instead of being proud of the direction my life was moving. This caused me to doubt the decisions I was making as my confidence began to diminish. I wrestled with feeling worthless and questioned the validity of my calling.

A conversation shared with a friend about publishing my first book and launching a ministry turned into one of the most hurtful conversations I've ever had to endure. She told me that not everyone is as lucky as I am to do the things I do. Anger bubbled up inside of me as I tried to process what I was hearing.

I wondered, "Is this what people feel about me?" To believe everything I had worked incredibly hard for and sacrificed so much of my time, money, and energy for was pure luck just didn't sit right with me. In that moment, my insecurities rose up. I took the entire conversation personally, but worked hard to not allow my emotions to cloud my judgment.

Withdrawn, I was extremely quiet after that conversation. I never confronted the person who said it, but I found myself disconnected from her more and more. The more I would dwell on the hurtful thing she said, the more I would think, "You are the lucky one; you have children, and I don't." I allowed the pain of infertility to resurface.

This took me on one giant negative spiral as I held a grudge against her—not for what she said—but for the mere fact that she was a mother and I wasn't. I had deduced that she couldn't possibly ever understand my decisions and circumstances because she hadn't suffered like I had. She couldn't possibly know that having a business made me feel like a mother as I nurtured and grew my business, while still grieving the loss of my children.

I wish I could say I came to my senses quickly, but like most hard lessons, this one seemed to linger. As time passed, I became extremely bitter about my situation. That's the thing with jealousy. If left unchecked and unresolved, it festers and grows into this giant angry ball in the pit of your stomach. My coping mechanism is to freeze when I feel challenged or hurt, and this interaction definitely froze me in place.

Shrinking even more, I stopped sharing parts of myself and my business with others for fear of the same thing happening again. I disconnected from attending gatherings that revolved around children because I was so bitter about not being able to have my own that I couldn't fully celebrate other people's children. This dampened my spirit and purpose and threatened to ruin everything I had worked so hard to build as I was publishing my book.

To be authentic, I needed to be comfortable sharing my struggles with infertility and the insensitivity I've encountered concerning my life choices. I continued to hold back, even though I replayed conversations with other women struggling with infertility who encouraged me to share more about my struggles and talk openly about everything. Bravery was something I lacked, and I realized how much I needed to change my heart if I wanted to be a great leader.

Holding onto bitterness and grudges and not forgiving others revealed a lack of love in my spirit. Instead of having an open discussion with my friend about how her comment made me feel, I allowed our jealousy towards each other to separate us as close friends. Although it was done out of respect for her feelings about how my life choices made her feel—once again keeping my mouth tightly shut created further damage. Though this didn't completely sever our relationship, it has affected it more than I would like.

Don't Be Ashamed

Infertility is another one of those unexpected circumstances that you cannot control, despite your best efforts. Women rarely talk about their feelings surrounding their infertility with others. It's just one of those things people don't talk about because their circumstance may embarrass them. I'm sure only those who have struggled with infertility understand this, but I am also fairly certain that most of my family and friends don't truly know the magnitude of emotions I carry being infertile, because I keep it to myself.

Not being open and honest about our feelings may create a division among friends who cannot put their differences aside long enough to accept each other as they are. Women may view each other as competition and sometimes have an uncanny need to beat each other at everything they do. Whether it's competing for a better job, fancier car, or more children, the driving force behind the need to be above one another grows more and more. This constant pitting against each other is exhausting. I believe this world would be far greater if we banded together to help one another succeed instead of pointing out each other's flaws as we claw our way to the top.

Perhaps I should have responded in a way that led with love and tried to understand why she felt I was lucky to have achieved all that I have. I would have discovered that she was far too exhausted to put time and attention into the things she wanted to do as she struggled with the demands of work, marriage, and children. All that she encounters daily may cause her to feel as though she has lost a little of herself. It could have been her cry for help as she felt herself slipping away despite the longing to do more.

Ashamed, I realized I unfairly carried this grudge against her for far too long. It was very wrong of me to respond in the manner I did. Thankfully, I have learned a much better approach to hard conversations like this. We can't take back what we said or did in the past, but we can grow and learn as we change how we react to better handle conflicts.

Perhaps I should have addressed the comments with my friend immediately and checked in to make sure she was doing okay. I now know this is the better approach and plan to be more open to reconciling differences gracefully. The thing I learned most about friendship is we often get extremely comfortable with the friends we enjoy most. This level of comfortability will sometimes come with the removal of filters as you speak what is on your mind instead of lovingly approaching a sensitive topic.

I often take criticism personally, but I am learning to look at it as an opportunity for growth rather than sitting in the pain. We are all different in how we approach difficult conversations that may point out insecurities others have without realizing it.

Value Your Relationships

I value my relationship with God more highly than I value my friendships—but my friends are still high on the list. Because I value them as highly as I do, I always hope to seek resolution where possible in all situations. When someone tells me something I am doing is causing them to struggle, I take it seriously. This doesn't mean I have to shrink who I am or what I am doing, but listen to why they are struggling and for the betterment of both of us. Sometimes that will require that I put a new boundary in place to remove discussion of that topic from future conversations.

Back when I constantly faced questions about having children, I wish I had realized to do this. Perhaps boundaries could have saved endless frustrating conversations and strained relationships if I would have set it in place earlier. I can't go back in time to make the switch, but I can keep this in mind moving forward with each new relationship I build.

Friendship is most successful with balance. If one side is constantly giving and the other is taking without replenishing, the imbalance of the friendship will eventually crack the foundation. If a friend upsets you, the best thing you can do is offer forgiveness, seek resolution, and let go of the grudges you were clinging to. Remember, your friend is human, just as you are. We all make mistakes, and while some mistakes are irreparable, most of them can be corrected.

Another great reminder is there are two very different people with very different feelings and beliefs in any given situation. Being respectful of each other shows how much you care about the other person. Lashing out in retaliation will only further separate you from your friend. We want to respond, not react.

A better response in my situation could have been to ask her why she felt the way she did about my situation. If I would have asked her to explain her stance, then offer my perspective, we would have been able to set the boundary in place without upsetting either of us anymore. We may have been able to come to a resolution immediately without causing a divide in our relationship that lasted far too long.

Friendships are something I enjoy as it gives me a chance to relax after a stressful week with someone I care about. By making sure I have boundaries that honor both of us, I can continue enjoying time spent with my friends instead of distancing myself when troubles may arise.

Due to working from home, I crave communication with others and when I have time to sit with someone in conversation, I feel like I have a lot of time to make up. Practicing self-control in these situations helps me to ensure I'm not unbalancing our friendship by offloading my baggage and not giving them a chance to offload theirs. If I sense hesitancy, I'll try to ask guiding questions to help them open up more.

Because I value my friendships, I have made a conscious effort not to unload all my thoughts on my friends at once. Instead, I carefully choose when to share. I'm open and honest about my struggles because I believe withholding them prevents others from truly understanding me. Likewise, I hope to instill a safe space for them to open up freely and share their struggles as well.

This level of communication is best handled among friends who are trustworthy with your secrets. Having been on both sides of gossip in the past, I know how hurtful it can be. Ensure your friends know they can trust you with matters of their heart, and that you will safeguard their confessions. The only exception to this rule is when someone may be potentially in danger.

A person's limitations in life do not define whether their life matters. Finding trusted friends who honor you by lifting you up when you are feeling down and whom you can do the same for helps make life a touch simpler. We all have battles hidden below the surface. Keep this in mind the next time one of your relationships is struggling. Check in with your friend to see if they are hurting and in need of comforting. Pray for them often and if they are open to it, offer to pray with them.

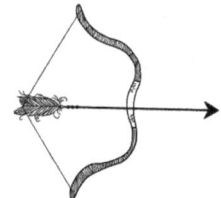

By changing how you approach your friendships, you are actively working on a better way to handle conflict with others.

With time, you'll strengthen your communication skills, which will help you become a stronger leader.

The Unseen Truth

I allowed the hurt from taking a comment too personally and allowing it to cloud my judgment of our friendship. My reaction came from a place of jealousy as I retaliated with thoughts about all the things she had, and I felt I was lacking and wished I had. Taking a position of defense, I shut down and withdrew from her instead of confronting the differences of opinions we had and setting healthy boundaries within our friendship.

Jealousy, if left to grow, can eventually turn into holding onto grudges as you push people away. One thing I always try to remind myself is, people only share the best side of things. But under the surface, there may be far more we can't see. There is so much work being done behind the scenes that leads people to their successes and achievements, often at a sacrifice to the person doing the work. You may wish you could have what they have, but you may not understand the price they have paid to have it.

We all live very different lives, have different beliefs, and take different actions. It is possible that the reason we are feeling jealous is actually in part to us discovering where we are lacking in our own quest to fulfill a goal. Is our response something that would make God proud of us, or would He look into our eyes and say, "My child, please remember that I love them too"?

Have you ever unfairly judged someone because of their circumstances and later held a grudge against them?

Braver with Belief

"Whoever would foster love covers over an offense, but whoever repeats the matter separates close friends."
Proverbs 17:9

In order to become braver with belief, we have to remember to lead in love in responding to those who hurt us. I recognize the difficulty in doing this and want to make sure I am clear in stating we are not to react in a way that is displeasing to the other person, but we respond in a way that is pleasing to God. As children, we learn to think before speaking, but as adults, we disregard caution and quickly blurt out whatever we think. This quick reaction can be the destruction of a relationship that ends badly.

Growing in faith teaches us the importance of discernment, forgiveness, and compassion, to name a few. When we accept the situation as it is and put aside our differences, we can clearly see how to respond properly in this type of situation. Naturally, looking back, I realize how I mishandled this situation and missed an opportunity to check in and make sure she was okay because this wasn't at all typical behavior for her.

Sometimes we have to put aside our pride to better understand our friend. For a friendship to remain strong, it takes work from both individuals. When you face a test of friendship, it is important to discuss how this test made both of you feel as you seek resolution. It is never advisable to react in a way that repeats the offense delivered to you, but to respond in love with reconciliation in mind.

Likewise, as you lead more, those who come to you for guidance will come to depend on you in a way that puts everything in a spotlight. This can feel intimidating—but by leading by example, you will further reinforce your teachings.

The Strength in Letting Go

I have wanted to be a mother for as long as I can remember. It is often difficult for me to feel as if I have fulfilled this desire despite having been a foster mom and enduring a miscarriage. I refused to accept my situation for a very long time, as it controlled my life obsessively. I took the medication despite having allergic reactions, took my temperature daily, logged every single detail, and planned out every chance I could get.

In all of it, the results were always the same gut-wrenching negative test that left me in a heap on the cold bathroom floor as I wailed. I eventually realized that if I were to have any chance of living a life I could enjoy, I had to first accept the fact I would never be a mother. Once I accepted it, I could then allow God the chance to show me what it was He wanted me to do with my life despite this disability.

With having a situation like infertility, losing a job, moving farther away from loved ones, or an autoimmune disease, often the results can be completely out of your hands. Remember that your unique situation creates a path forward that may look different from your friends. It is your decision, and yours alone, how you handle it. Understand that others cannot always sympathize with you if they have never gone through what you are facing. You can apply the same principle to how you handle others' differing choices.

Let go of the bitterness you hold for those living a seemingly "normal" life compared to yours.

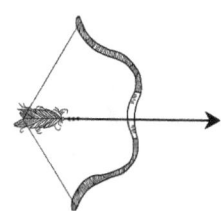

Don't let jealousy consume you when others receive the blessings you crave. Focus on you and your relationship with God during this season of your life.

Choose to do something that brings joy and purpose back into your heart. You do not need to explain your choices to anyone; they are yours to make.

Does it feel like nobody understands you or your circumstances? For me, it feels like this more times than I care to admit. The next time someone hurts your feelings about how you are currently living your life or a situation you are going through; I want to encourage you to look at it from their perspective and not just your own. When you respond, do so from a place of love and compassion, and not out of hurt. You may just discover that they are coming from a hurt place and need your help to heal.

Moving Forward with Hope

Even if life for you doesn't bring forth children—or any other thing you feel is missing—your life still matters. There are extremely fulfilling things you can do outside of what you envisioned. This doesn't mean the grief of this loss goes away. It will always be there, but it means that you can choose to live life again as you give birth to many new ideas with God's guidance. We must also choose to overcome regret if we hope to move forward in a way that honors God. I will cover this in our next chapter.

Braver Choices

Actionable steps you can take to become braver with belief as you step into the role of servant leader. I have broken it down for you in a way that is easier to remember: B.R.A.V.E.R.

Brighten: An action taking call to service to refine our hearts as we discover the area in which to serve.

Serving Others: Explore ways you can start something new that benefits others. This could be volunteering for a local charity, offering to babysit for a single mother, or any other act of kindness that is manageable for you.

Reflect: A prayer that covers the emotions felt within each chapter with a promise to let go of the things we need to, so we can keep moving forward.

> *Father, I am so sorry I didn't respond in love. Help me let go of the bitterness I harbor against others out of jealousy. Please forgive me for allowing grudges to take root and separate me from my close friends. Amen.*

Act: An action taking exercise that forces us to get up and move forward.

Repair a slightly cracked but still repairable friendship damaged by your grudge. Reach out, seek forgiveness, and work together towards reconciliation.

Verse: Memorization of a Bible verse that helps us remember the lesson within the chapter.

Write the following scripture and post it somewhere you'll see it every day; maybe a bathroom mirror, refrigerator, or your home office. Memorize it and refer to it when you feel jealousy begin to creep in.

"And when you stand praying, if you hold anything against anyone, forgive them, so that your Father in heaven may forgive you your sins."

Mark 11:25

Explore: An action taking exercise to help us explore new possibilities we may not have yet thought of.

Write a statement of decision: I choose to let go of [insert grudge] because I no longer want to carry the weight of resentment. I am choosing peace and forgiveness.

Renew: A journal prompt for us to reflect with God in solitude.

Journal Prompt: Focus on a grudge you hold that has had lingering effects. In your journal, answer this question—How has holding this grudge affected my relationship with God?

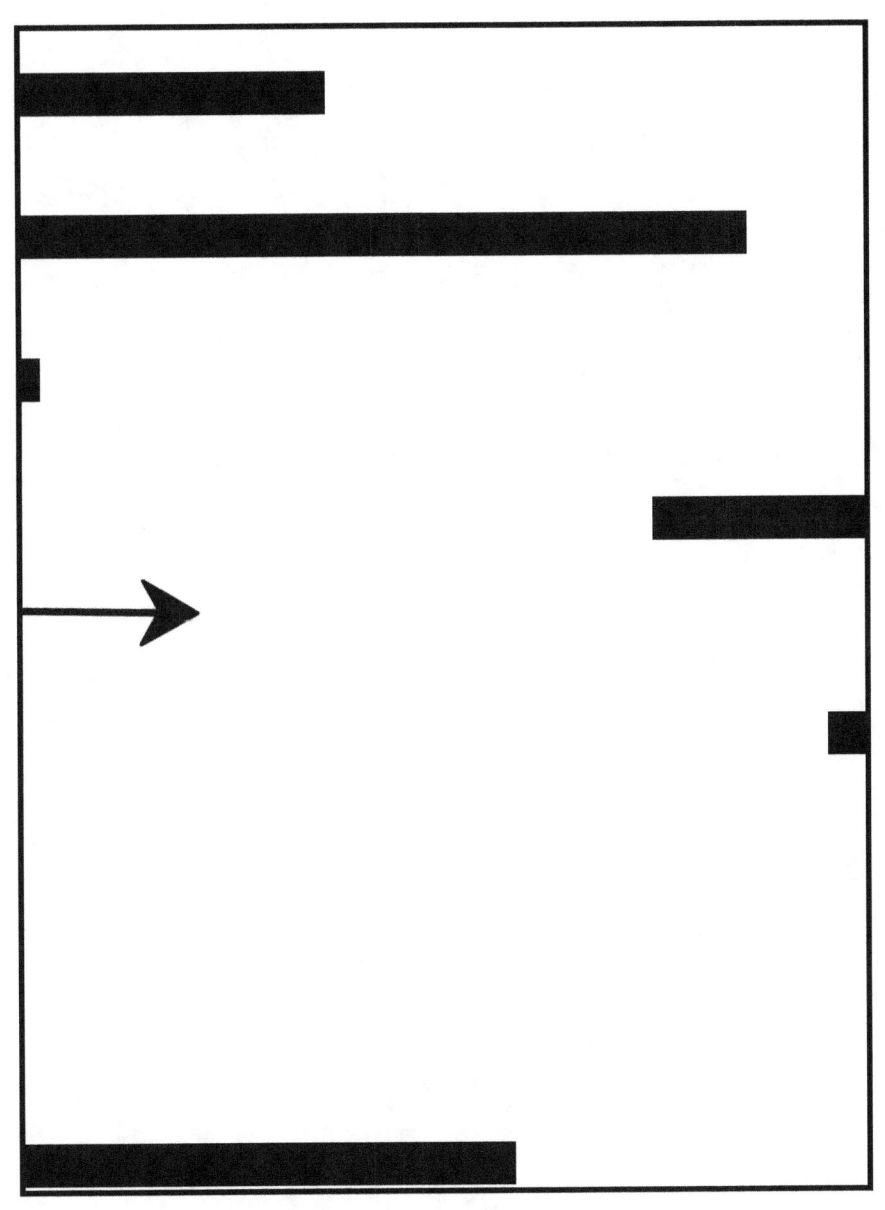

chapter Three

Overcoming Regret

Letting go of grudges was significant in opening my heart up to discover the things I was still holding onto far too tightly. I have always been an overthinker, analyzing things I've said or done repeatedly until I'm exhausted. Once I let go of the grudges, my mind was freed up to focus on something else. Fortunately for me, it was yet another lesson I desperately needed to continue on my way of being braver with belief so I could become a more capable servant leader.

With a fresh perspective, I discovered something new: regret had now taken up residence in my heart. It spread out as far as it could, claiming its space and prohibiting forgiveness from holding its rightful space. The enemy will use regret as a tool to keep us right where he wants us. As long as we play scenarios on repeat in our mind, we don't allow room for conversation with God to enter.

I desperately wanted the chance to change, to become the woman God was creating me to be, and I knew the only way this could happen was to evict regret from my heart. Only one question remained: how do I get rid of regret once and for all?

Feeling Helpless

I held my breath as I stared at my body in the mirror over our double vanity in the bathroom. Taking in everything, I saw in my reflection and exhaled. Frustrated with the woman staring back at me, I forced myself to pay attention to every single detail. As I turned from side to side, I grabbed the rolls that collected at my waistline and seemed to continue to grow. A deep sense of sorrow and regret bubbled up inside, and I forced myself to choke back the sobs that threatened to escape. I have struggled with weight my whole life, but at one time, I had been doing so well and was in great physical shape. What happened between then and now?

When I go back in time to pinpoint when the weight packed on again, I can trace it to my time spent at the beginning in 2017. I was at the bottom of the ocean, feeling as if I'd lost my identity. After my miscarriage, I didn't have the strength to take care of myself like I used to. Giving up on myself, I'd sunk to the ocean floor and developed an unhealthy habit: negative self-talk. Every time I looked in the mirror, I started repeating all the mean things people said about my appearance over the years. Through repetition, I came to believe it. And in believing it, I became it.

Perhaps I'll never understand why appearance so heavily influences how others treat a person. My weight has fluctuated throughout my life, and I've been treated in dramatically different ways depending on whether I was thinner or overweight.

For the longest time, I tried everything I could to get thin again. But each time, I only ended up making my situation far worse than where I had started. Skipping meals and limiting diets had been the one path that led to thinness, but not healthiness. It took me a long time to fully overcome anorexia, and I was determined to never do it that way again.

Just before I had given up on myself, I had spent a slight fortune on products recommended to me by my fertility healthcare team. I followed the plan precisely. Imagine my surprise and disappointment when, on the day I had to weigh in, I had gained fifteen pounds instead of losing anything.

My doctor was certain I must have lied on my meal logs because, in her mind, my weight gain was all the evidence she needed. After three months with the same results, I weighed even more than when I started, and my mindset had taken a huge nosedive. I refused to spend another dime on the supplements I had been buying from them because I had all the proof I needed to know they simply didn't work for me.

Overwhelmed by my latest experience, I fixated on all the regrets I was carrying. I regretted so many things—failed relationships, lost jobs, having to say goodbye to our foster children, and never being able to lose enough weight to get pregnant and carry to full term. The amount of regret weighed so heavily that it only contributed to my growing waistline; I stopped paying attention to the food I put in my body and the chemicals that were in the products I used.

My doctor's dismissive attitude toward me only added to my frustration. I knew I would have to take matters into my own hands—and yet I did absolutely nothing.

A couple years later, a photograph was taken of me at an event and posted on social media. Looking at that photograph, I felt so embarrassed. In an effort to take action, I ran head first into another supplement plan a friend had shared with me without fully researching the ingredients for myself. The supplements helped for a short time when paired with fasting, but eventually, the same problem happened as weight wouldn't budge and increased again.

During a routine procedure with my digestive care team, I was advised to stop all supplements, as the ingredients in them were questionable in terms of how they were interacting with my body. My digestive tract needed a break. I left that appointment discouraged and filled with regret over my decision to try the supplemental route again. I knew I had issues with certain foods, so it had been a complete waste of time and money with nothing to show for it.

In 2020, things got tricky for me as the foods I knew worked well for me became hard to find. As a result, I was eating food I knew I shouldn't consume. In some things, I felt I had no other choice as I needed a well-rounded diet to survive. Eventually, things returned to normal, and I had become more resourceful in the process, finding alternative places to get food through local farm co-ops.

While I didn't lose a large amount of weight, I did lose some—and that gave me the hope to continue in the direction I was going. I coasted through to the end of 2023, when my stress levels became unacceptably high. I struggled with bloating, low energy, and generally feeling unwell. I desperately needed a change—any change at all.

In January 2024, the year I started writing this book, I became extremely ill. This wasn't just a cold that would get better with time. It was debilitating pain, fever, nausea, digestive upset, and body tremors every night.

The timing of this illness could not have been worse, not just because of the severity of the situation, but because it was Mike's birthday. We usually celebrate the entire week by doing things he enjoys. My condition certainly put a damper on our celebration plans, and I felt horrible for it.

A full week of being sick depleted my immune system. I pushed through a church service as best I could, but as soon as we got back home, I collapsed in bed to rest. It had taken every ounce of energy I had left. A liquid diet became necessary to help my digestion heal because eating was unbearably painful.

I dismissed my symptoms, certain this could be attributed to my autoimmune disease. Gradually I began to recover to the point I could tolerate food a little more, but I wasn't fully recovering. Eventually, I met with my digestive team, who scheduled further testing that uncovered I had diverticulitis.

Regret flooded my mind as I began to better understand the diagnosis. My body was crying out for me to take better care of it. There was no more time to put things off. I had a lot of work to do to help my body heal.

February 2024 | Reality Check

The follow up appointment after my diagnosis terrified me. My doctor had given me literature on how to prevent another flare up of diverticulitis and informed me that diverticulosis was a condition I would have for the rest of my life. I read horror stories in my own research of what could happen if I didn't take this diagnosis seriously and make some major lifestyle changes.

Despite working hard to improve my overall health the year before, I was surprised to learn how unwell I had become. In addition to the reality of my diagnosis, another reality emerged: I had far too much stress in my life, and in order to get better, I needed to reduce it.

For several weeks, I prayed for wisdom to make the best health-altering choice. Elevated cholesterol and blood sugar levels were also found during my annual blood work and increased my list of health problems. Accepting responsibility for my current situation required acknowledging my extended period of self-abandonment. To improve my health, I had to admit I needed the help of a professional. After our discussion, my primary care team recommended I work with a dietician.

I chose a dietician with experience dealing with complex cases like mine. Most dietitians are trained to focus on weight loss. Her plan needed to help me focus on getting healthier overall.

I had to remind myself that my body was my temple, and in order to honor God, I had to take much better care of it than I had been. In the first session with my new dietician, I was forced to confront parts of myself that I had buried deep as she asked me questions about my past eating disorder and current thoughts of my body image.

In one of the hardest conversations I've had, I confessed how ashamed I was for the current state my body was in and my embarrassment about how large I had become. It meant so much to me when she told me what matters the most is making choices now to improve my overall health and not to focus so much on what the numbers are saying. Unlike other medical professionals, she was not focused strictly on my weight.

The first two weeks after that appointment, I worked on things internally to make sure my mindset was in a place where I could successfully make changes without sabotaging my progress.

The next step was in testing for food sensitivities and allergies through blood work and an elimination protocol diet. She warned me this was extremely difficult and I would likely want to give up, but reminded me what I was doing was going to be so good for my overall health and wellness. She was right. I struggled the first three weeks with only being able to eat twenty foods, especially because some were things

I didn't like. The elimination protocol diet is one of the harder things I have gone through.

It was difficult to give up coffee, sugar, and, most of all, sauces. Try eating a dry bowl of plain lettuce and tell me how much you like it! At the time, I definitely questioned my life choices. But now, I regret not having done this much sooner.

The process with my dietician is ongoing as I am writing this. I have been successfully doing the elimination protocol diet now for eight months. I have found what foods are safe for me to consume and what foods I really need to avoid. There were also food allergies I didn't know I had.

I've lost over forty pounds, which, for me, is a miracle in itself. Some weight loss is also because of understanding the importance of a balanced nutritional plate, and eliminating foods that caused added inflammation in my body. I also contribute weight loss to finally treating my body as God intended, which has made me far healthier than I've ever been before.

At our latest meeting, my dietician asked me what I want to work on next, now that I have a handle on what I can and cannot eat. Knowing the importance of exercise, especially as I continue to age, I want to keep my body strong and healthy for as long as possible. I told her that in my laziness, I stopped exercising—and it used to be something I genuinely enjoyed doing and I wanted to get back into.

With her help, we devised a plan to incorporate exercise into my wellness plan. I heard her when she told me to give grace to myself and not be so hard on myself if I miss a day of working out. The goal was to work on forming new habits that include making exercise a priority.

In the past, I had always been hard on myself if I missed a scheduled workout. My thoughts lingered after our call, as I debated whether I should even schedule the workouts. This led me to believe our plan would probably lead to failure and disappointment. Instead, I made it my goal to work in two days of exercise to start each week until I built myself up to my end goal of weight training when my body was ready to tolerate it.

To be frank, I failed to uphold my end of the plan, which only added to the growing regret I had within. My dietician encouraged me to wait until after the holidays to begin this new exercise plan, but I was so determined to make it work during the holidays. For me, it was another classic case of putting too big of an expectation on myself without considering my realistic timeline. With the busy holiday season, it is difficult for me to add exercise into my routine. I got some workouts in, but not nearly enough to create a new consistent habit.

Release the Weight

I've made some mistakes in my life that I've regretted. Most of them I can chalk up to immaturity, desperation, or wanting to belong somewhere. At the time I made those choices, it felt right for the situation I was in. However, when it went awry, I would beat myself up repeatedly and tell myself how stupid I was for making that decision. I now view these as learning opportunities as I file them away in my 'what not to do again' files.

Regret comes in various forms. Maybe you regret missed opportunities, making poor choices, not living an authentic life, or not pursuing your passions. Perhaps your life has gone in such a way that you've picked up regrets and continued to carry them with you.

Having the bravery to say, "I messed up, and I want to do better," is the first step in overcoming everything that is holding you back. Do you find yourself picking up the weighted bag of regret and continuing to carry it? Think of how much more you could achieve with a fresh start and a lighter load.

The story I shared with you in this chapter was chosen because I know many of my friends struggle with their self-image the same way I have and I think it will resonate with many of you, too. Self-image is something I have struggled with for so long, I can't even remember the event that started it.

Closing my eyes, I pictured myself dragging this giant heavy bag around with me. Though I believed I was progressing toward my goal, when I paused in my tracks, it revealed I'd only circled my bag, creating a ground indentation mirroring my directionless path.

If I continue dragging the weight of regret behind me, I will never give myself the chance I need to make the lifestyle changes my body deserves. Only by releasing what binds me can I escape this fruitless path.

I will no longer live my life regretting unkindness to my body, mind, or soul.

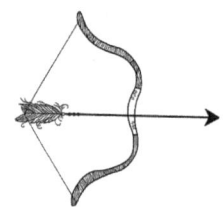

Recognizing the need for more gentleness and realistic self-expectations, I find myself in a new place: my goal isn't to have a perfect body, but a healthy one that will help me serve others for a long time.

Once I stopped criticizing myself, I was able to start working on the problem with a new outlook.

The way forward is to let go of the past, forgive myself for the mistakes I've made, learn from them, and grow into the best possible version of myself. It is by choosing this path, I hope to inspire others and teach them to meet themselves where they are.

If your body image is the very thing you continually struggle with, a closer look into your mindset on the subject may help. Are you focused purely on the desire to be thin and well put-together, or is it overall health and wellbeing you seek? Whichever way you answer this question, the first step to achieving your goals is to approach yourself with the kindness you would have in speaking to a friend. I would also encourage you to seek out your ideal medical care team to aid you in uncovering what is best for you and your body. It is worth the effort.

Keep in mind we are all very different, and what I have found to work for me may not work for you and vice versa. It is important that as you work on the physical attributes you have, that you do not compare your progress to the progress of others.

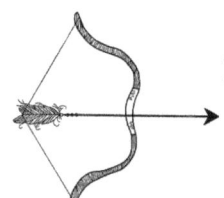

Be only in competition with who you were yesterday as you work towards becoming a better version of yourself today.

Whatever regret you are holding onto, consider the consequences of continuing to walk around and around it. Every time you beat yourself up for making a poor choice, you are adding more weight to the bag. We are often the hardest on ourselves because we don't trust that we can improve our situation. Could it be that you don't trust you can improve because you haven't given yourself the chance to prove you can?

What's done is done. You cannot take it back, you can't change it, and you are unfortunately stuck with the consequences of the decisions you made. It feels overwhelming to consider the possibility of accepting those consequences because they usually aren't pleasant.

I know you want your situation to improve immediately. Sadly, that isn't how growth works. You can improve your situation over time, but only if you take that first step to initiate a change so big that it can alter the course you're on.

I know you have what it takes within you to make this change happen.

If you feel stuck where you are now, pause and look up. Have you been walking in a circle around your bag of regret? It is time to release the weight regret has been adding to your life.

The Unseen Truth

I recognized by holding onto too many years of regret, I was contributing to the unhealthy state my body, mind, and soul had become. This hard realization had the power to either cause me to continue in a self-destructive state, or completely change my actions for improvement. I recognized I needed professional help, and for the first time in my life, I prioritized that need and my health. In doing so, I created new habits that have long-lasting effects on my overall wellbeing.

Instead of continuing to spread myself too thin by overbooking my schedule, I now scheduled things in a way that prioritized my health. At first, I felt guilty for putting myself first when I said no to joining others in meals out. Once I saw the benefit of changing my diet and lifestyle, I could drop the guilt as I picked up peace in my choice for treating my temple more kindly.

The regret you carry may not be the same as the regret I carry, but the lesson remains: once you let go of regret, you can allow God to work in your life in new ways that have long-lasting outcomes. This shift helps you in developing habits that enhance your mind, body, and soul as you put in the work of becoming the best version of yourself that you can be.

What regrets are you holding onto that are adding unnecessary weight to your life?

Braver with Belief

"Forget the former things; do not dwell on the past. See, I am doing a new thing! Now it springs up; do you not perceive it? I am making a way in the wilderness and streams in the wasteland."
Isaiah 43:18-19

In order to become braver with belief, we need to look forward to the new things springing up instead of dwelling on the past. Those *shoulda, woulda, coulda* moments are only adding to your constant state of regret. Acknowledging the choices you made are what brought you to where you are today is the first step in overcoming the regret of not having made better choices. The more you deny that there was a problem in the choices you made, the more regret keeps adding to you.

Once you identify the areas you fell short, it is important to extend grace to yourself for deciding how you did. We all make mistakes. It's how we learn and grow as we adapt and change. What is done is done. It belongs in the past while you move forward to a brighter future. If the situation you find yourself in feels impossible to work through, I want to remind you how brave you are. Do what you need to do to keep moving.

We can sum up exactly what's needed at this very moment in one word: change. I know, I know, that word is terrifying. Trust me, I get it and I agree with you. Change is so hard—but it is also imperative if you want to continue to grow and develop as a human. By choosing to go all in on improving the areas in which you are struggling, you are making a conscious effort to align yourself with God's vision for your life. Once you do this, He will begin to reveal to you the reason behind the choices you made, and how you can use your experiences to help someone else through theirs. Your past doesn't define you, but it helps shape you. You become a better leader when you can find the growth that happened during the trials.

The Strength in Letting Go

I have longed to be different than I was my whole life, instead of accepting how God created me. Rather than making the changes I needed to make, I wasted an extraordinary amount of time and energy simply wishing things were different. I found myself in the perpetual loop of hating what I saw in the mirror, while comparing myself to others and wishing my body would look like theirs. By comparing myself to others, I wasn't allowing myself the chance to learn more about my body and what it can or cannot handle. Once I sought help in this area, I could then get the help I needed to initiate changes that helped me give myself grace and learn to love myself again.

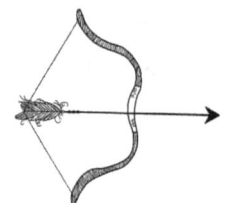 **When you overcome the regret you harbor, you are free to move forward into all that God has waiting for you.**

While it is good to be mindful of your health and wellbeing, it is unhealthy to be fixated on all the things you dislike about your body. This negativity keeps you hyper fixated on something as a distraction to keep you from working towards what God is calling you to do. For instance, if I continued believing no one would listen to me because of my weight, I would remain silent instead of actively teaching others about God's goodness.

I didn't just let go of regret, I said hello to loving and understanding my body, mind, and soul a bit more. There was a massive shift from *I can't*, to *I have to try* that naturally occurred. The severity of the situation I had found myself in meant I had no other choice but to change if I wanted to continue to live a long and healthy life. As a result, I met myself where I was, gave love and acceptance of who I am, and opened my heart to receive the lessons God was revealing to me.

Let go of the regrets you clutch onto as if your life depends on it—because it does. Look your past mistakes square in the face and acknowledge that you messed up. Immediately create a plan you can put into place and take action now toward bettering your life and situation. As you look back at these areas you are letting go, ask yourself, what is one lesson you can take from your experiences?

Does it feel like the weight of regrets is crushing you underneath? For me, I know I couldn't breathe as my reality came face to face with the choices of my past. The good news is, you've just recognized the need for change. All you have to do now is take that first step to a better you.

Moving Forward with Hope

Being brave enough to initiate change in your life is admirable. Seek God's direction, wisdom, and patience as you put a new plan in place to work on you. Be honest with family and friends about what you are working towards and firm when you say no to things that will slow your progress. You'll find that they'll likely encourage you more than they'll discourage you. You are doing a great job so far! Keep it up. In the next chapter, we are going to tackle the importance of forgiveness and how we can get there.

Braver Choices

Actionable steps you can take to become braver with belief as you step into the role of servant leader. I have broken it down for you in a way that is easier to remember: B.R.A.V.E.R.

Brighten: An action taking call to service to refine our hearts as we discover the area in which to serve.

Serving Yourself: Choose an area you feel you have neglected and improve it.

Reflect: A prayer that covers the emotions felt within each chapter with a promise to let go of the things we need to, so we can keep moving forward.

> *Father, I am so sorry I have been carrying around regret for so long. Help me let go of regret as I work on bettering myself. Please forgive me for negatively speaking to myself as I struggled to face my past mistakes. Amen.*

Act: An action taking exercise that forces us to get up and move forward.

Spend time in solitude. Close your eyes, take deep slow breaths to calm your mind. Repeat the following: "I forgive myself for [what you are regretting] and release the weight of regret."

Verse: Memorization of a Bible verse that helps us remember the lesson within the chapter.

Write the following scripture and post it somewhere you'll see it every day; maybe a bathroom mirror, refrigerator, or your home office. Memorize it and refer to it when you are feeling shame and regret.

"Godly sorrow brings repentance that leads to salvation and leaves no regret, but worldly sorrow brings death."
2 Corinthians 7:10

Explore: An action taking exercise to help us explore new possibilities we may not have yet thought of.

Visual Exercise: Close your eyes and visualize yourself standing with an extremely heavy bag. You drag it with you as you walk to a more peaceful place—perhaps a beach, forest, or garden—and you set the bag down. Watch as you open up the bag and face what you have carried with you for so long. See yourself turning and walking away from the bag as you continue forward, feeling lighter and more at peace. Because we are human, we will still wonder what happens to the bag. To squash this sense of wonder, pause, turn and look as Jesus picks up your bag and carries it away for you. Give Him thanks, turn back around, and keep walking forward, feeling lighter and lighter as you go.

Renew: A journal prompt for us to reflect with God in solitude.

Journal Prompt: How do I feel now that I have let go of the weight of regret?

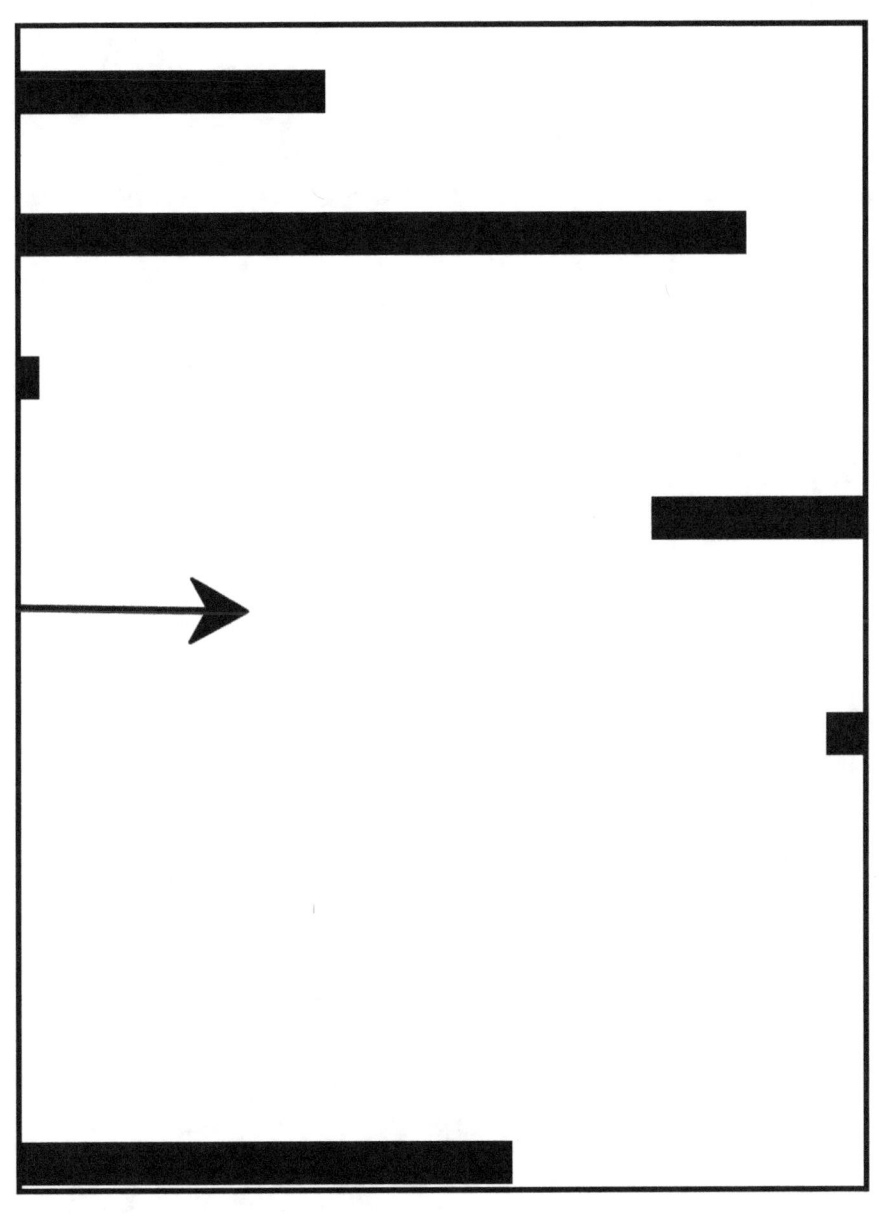

Chapter Four

Path to Forgiveness

Being free to move forward into all God has waiting for me also made me realize something was still holding me back. It's never enough to overcome regret without first forgiving yourself for what brought you to regret.

While I no longer regretted the decisions I made thus far, I could still feel the hurt that surrounded them. When I should have been my biggest advocate and supporter, I felt I let myself down time and time again.

As I let go of the need to overanalyze why I felt let down, I could start to work on learning to forgive myself. Yet something told me this would be much harder than forgiving someone else for hurting me.

We are often quick to extend forgiveness for the transgressions caused by our friends and family—but when faced with our own transgressions, we are often unable to extend that same grace to ourselves.

August 2024 | Becoming Braver

I held on to disappointment for so long I had forgotten why I was mad at myself. Has this ever happened to you? I have to admit, I am my worst critic and harshest judge. I'm known for beating myself up over mistakes and failures, especially if I feel I've been careless.

Becoming braver is something I was certain would also make me more confident as I became more resilient. I have always had an instinct to protect myself the best I could from getting hurt too badly from others, yet the way I treated myself was a completely different story. My self-criticism and judgment had become a problem.

There is a fine line between striving to be a better human being and actually doing the work to become one. As my heart hardened with each disappointment, I knew I wanted to be different than I had become. Worried I would always stay this way, I was determined to change. The constant negativity left me exhausted and unhappy. I could clearly see toxic traits and patterns I had picked up and clung to for much longer than I should have.

If only I could tell you I magically changed one day and never looked back. But I can't tell you this, because it isn't true. What I believe happened was a refining of my heart and a renewing of spirit as I continually sought time with God daily. I prayed, asking Him to uncover what was causing me to be so critical. Over time, my prayers grew more detailed, yet comfortable, as I relaxed in the presence of God. I could sense He was helping me peel back each hardened layer around my heart as He lovingly, yet firmly, showed me areas I needed to improve upon.

On days when I could feel negativity creeping in, I challenged myself to correct my attitude as soon as I realized what I was doing. This is still a work in progress, as I am not yet perfect at self-realization. I often miss the mark on days I don't feel well. I try to remind myself that we all have bad days, but also try to respond instead of reacting on days my mood might be problematic.

There are many outside factors and triggers happening every single day which threaten to alter my mood in one quick second. Part of becoming a better human being means that when this happens, I need to be ready to recognize it and not allow it to be the driving force behind ruining someone else's day or my own. We are all battling things unseen. The last thing I want to do is make it harder for myself or for others.

Trying to change your ways after being the same way for a long time can be purely exhausting. The harder I tried, the crankier I became—and I needed a reset to occur fast. With the demands of my business, growing client project list, and my social calendar suddenly being filled to the max, I needed an escape.

In August of 2024, we went on a much-needed vacation to my favorite place, Hilton Head Island, South Carolina. This is my home away from home, a place I visited as a child, and where Mike and I got married. The last time we visited was in 2019, and we were long overdue for a beach vacation. Initially, we were going to take our RV there, but after the whole tornado incident, we changed our minds and booked a condo and drove. This allowed us the chance to enjoy our stay and relax as much as possible.

The first day on the beach, I immediately remembered why I love this place so much. I stood at the water's edge as the cool waves rushed in over my feet, staring off into the distance where the horizon disappeared. Standing there, I remembered my time spent at the bottom of the ocean, and gave thanks for being firmly planted on shore, unable to be thrown back in.

With the warm salty ocean air and gentle sound of the waves, I relaxed and allowed my thoughts to drift to where I was in life currently. Something was still missing, which created a feeling of unhappiness. Aware of the swimsuit I donned, I silently berated myself for not losing more weight before vacation. Looking down, I smoothed the fabric of my skirt over my hips, noticing the suit fit better than last year and was now looser in places. However, I couldn't help but feel a little sad realizing how unkind I had become to myself.

This realization was something that kept nagging at me every day we were on vacation. I wasn't beating myself up; rather, it alerted me to a behavior that was less than ideal. Reflecting on my younger self, I questioned whether I'd speak to her as I speak to myself now. I don't mean in the audible sense, but in my thoughts, particularly those when I would look at myself in the mirror or did or said something I wish I hadn't. Often, I would dwell on my past actions and long to change those moments.

This inability to be accepting of my own actions became permission to scold myself. I don't recall when I started doing this, or why I started doing it—but I know I have been doing it for a long time. It has almost become second nature to express disdain as I point out every flaw I have.

My thoughts swirled as my toes sank deeper in the sand and the ocean water rushed over my feet. Would I ever get to a point in my life where I could love the woman I have become?

Halfway through our trip, we booked a dolphin cruise. Excitement filled me as I bounded down the pier towards the boat. Fully aware of my physical size, I spotted a spot on the end where I wanted to sit to allow enough room for the other passengers. To my pleasant surprise, I easily walked between benches without having to turn sideways. As we took our seats on the boat, I quickly slipped on my motion sickness bands and got as comfortable as I could. I was grateful there weren't many of us on the cruise and we could spread out a bit more than usual.

The last time we took this cruise, we didn't see many dolphins because a hurricane was coming in and the water was incredibly choppy. The captain of the ship only took us around the local channels, and we didn't get to go out very far. I hoped this cruise would make up for the lack of dolphins on that one.

Now, I must share, dolphins are my favorite animal and have been since I was sixteen, thanks to this island. I giggled and squealed like I was the same sixteen year old girl again as the dolphins jumped up out of the water all around us. There were so many, I didn't know which side of the boat to look on. I took countless photos and videos to make sure I captured the moment the best I could. At one point, I decided I had enough footage to last a lifetime, and I walked to the back of the ship and sat next to Mike to soak it all in.

As the boat sped up, the wind whipped my hair across my face as the sun beat down on us. There was water all around us. It was a beautiful day, and despite the fun adventure, I found myself filled with sorrow. It was a moment of conviction I really needed, as I heard God gently nudge me to remember my sixteen year old self on my first dolphin cruise where I got to touch a dolphin. Sadness washed over me as I realized I had been unkind to her all these years later as I criticized my reflection in the mirror that very morning.

How much of my life had I spent being a bully to myself? I questioned why it was acceptable to speak this way to myself when I wouldn't speak this way to any of my friends. I knew immediately that it all had to stop. This would be the first step in becoming the woman God called me to be. Sitting there, I prayed, apologizing to God for my lack of self-compassion. I asked for forgiveness, and He reminded me I also needed to forgive myself.

At first, I tried to argue the step of forgiving myself was unnecessary, but in the end, I realized it was exactly what I needed. It's not a conversation you have with yourself in a way that you would another person. It's a thought you have where you admit all the terrible things you feel you've done that have contributed to your negative mindset. After I admitted all the things I had done, I accepted that I had forgiven myself for those actions and vowed to work harder at being kinder. It was in this inner work I felt a shift in perspective like I had never felt before.

I enjoyed the rest of the boat ride back to Harbour Town, and as the lighthouse came back to view, I felt like I was coming back home a changed woman. The next day, I put this recent change to the test as I again looked at myself in the mirror in my swimsuit. It was the first time I noticed how different my body looked after having lost the amount of weight I had: twenty-five pounds. I smiled at my reflection and whispered, "*I'm so proud of you.*"

Friend or Foe?

For the rest of the trip, I could fully relax and enjoy everything we did. I looked forward to the trip back home and felt ready to dive back into work, having taken the time to become fully rejuvenated. There had been a shift naturally occurring in my daily prayer time as I felt lighter and more free. With this new perspective, I felt it was time to prepare myself for a life in ministry.

Every time I had tried to get to this point, I always failed. As reminders of my shortcomings would find their way in and cause me to stumble backwards, I decided I simply wasn't ready. To prove my readiness, I decided the best approach was to maximize my learning before proceeding. I started absorbing as much as possible on leading a women's ministry; reading books, watching videos, and seeking mentors.

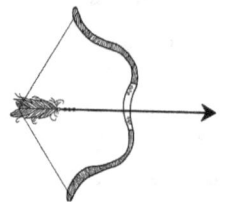

Because I had conquered one of the hardest things yet—forgiving myself—I knew I would succeed.

Unshackled from regret and shame, I was being kinder to myself than I had ever been because of having received forgiveness. I recognize when my thoughts shift back into old patterns and catch myself before I misspeak.

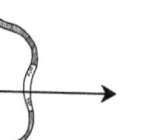

Negative self-talk, I believe, was the enemy's tool to keep me mentally captive.

It's a tactic still being used against me today, but because I have become braver with belief, I can stop the tactic before it is unleashed.

Take some time to consider the manner in which you speak to yourself. Be honest as you answer this question—are you your friend or a foe? This question is hard to answer, forcing you to examine your self-perception. For most of my life, I was my worst enemy, undermining my self-esteem by joining others in criticizing my flaws and appearance.

I never considered the possibility of being my friend instead. By choosing to be your friend, you are making the choice to be kinder, more gentle in your approach, and more loving in your actions. You let go of the desire to be your own worst enemy as you become your biggest cheerleader. Suddenly, life doesn't seem so hard and lonely because you know you have the strength to get through anything.

Once you decide which side you want to fall on—if you desire to be your friend instead of your foe—the first step you need to take is to forgive yourself for everything you've been mad at yourself for. For the bad choices you've made, the ideas you deemed were stupid, the unhealthy food you've shoveled into your body, the constant need to push yourself too hard, for not allowing yourself a chance to rest, or any other thing you are scolding yourself for. Let it go, fully, without hesitation, without looking back, and step forward a changed person—the person God authentically created you to be.

Fully Forgiven

Being able to move forward after forgiving my shortcomings has allowed me to view things from a different perspective. I'm not as hard on myself as I once was and likewise, I am also not critical of others. Failure to forgive ourselves for past mistakes prevents us from fully serving others with an open heart, because our hearts remain burdened by the past. Once you free up the space within, you peel back another hard layer of the exterior, which gives way to a much softer you.

When there is caution in serving others, it is usually driven from a past hurt, reminding you if you do this nice thing for someone, they will hurt you eventually. The constant reminder of how you feel you messed up by trying to do something kind is dredging up the past repeatedly. By forgiving them and yourself for contributing to the pain caused by that incident, you release it fully, which opens a way for you to try again. When you choose to serve others, do so without expectation of anything in return and with an open heart and mind because you want to do it.

Let's consider another area of forgiveness that is common for most people. If you have a friendship gone awry and you can't seem to let go of the ending of the friendship as you continually replay your last exchange, how can you find closure? Offering forgiveness to your friend for the part they played in the exchange is a good place to start. However, it simply isn't enough to help you close out that chapter. Forgive yourself for the part you also played in the exchange and what you did or didn't do afterwards. Let that relationship go and open up space for you to meet new people who fulfill your circle positively.

Forgiveness is something you cannot do on your own, but with help from God. It is important to remember why forgiveness is so integral to who you are and how it is an example of your relationship with God. If you are struggling to forgive yourself or others, this is an opportunity for you to draw closer to God. Ask Him for help in this area; it's okay to admit you cannot do it alone—and it's better to acknowledge this is a shortcoming you have and would like to improve upon.

Bitterness about a given situation may make forgiving yourself feel impossible. I remember prior to extending forgiveness to myself, I felt unlovable, broken in a way few others were. Before I could get to a place of forgiving myself, I first sought forgiveness from God. I desperately wanted to remove bitterness from my life and would do anything it took to see it through. Seeking forgiveness from God in prayer initially gave me the courage to extend forgiveness to others and eventually to myself.

When you view yourself as broken into a million pieces, you don't believe you can ever become whole again. Friend, God can and will make you whole again. But first, ask for His help in doing this. It sounds like a simple thing, to ask Him for help, but we both know it's not nearly as easy to do when we stand in our own way. Do you want to be made whole again?

Living Again

The feeling you get when you first confess your sins to God and seek forgiveness as you dedicate your life to Him is indescribable. I was sixteen when I received salvation, and I had a deep hunger to shout from the rooftops about God's goodness to everyone I encountered. With time, this feeling grew more distant as I discovered how harsh life could be. I have felt completely lost for the last few years, despite knowing distinctly whose I am and for whom I am living.

Many things challenged my faith as I questioned its validity and truth. Ultimately, I kept coming back because the one constant I felt through it all was that God still loved me. He allowed me the freedom to seek my truth and make my own decisions, no matter how far off they may have been. Despite repeatedly leaving Him, He never left me. Patiently and lovingly, He waited for my return.

The more I searched, the more I struggled with fully understanding the power of forgiveness. In the past, I tried forgiving others for hurting me, but even that was unsuccessful because I didn't fully forgive them. I had to learn to completely let go of the situation and keep no record of wrongs to move forward with forgiving them.

In my findings, it has historically been easier for me to forgive others than it was to forgive myself. I realized if I want to fully serve others, I must go down the path to forgiveness that would lead to a face-off with myself. It doesn't end there. The real challenge lies in what happens next. Choosing to be kinder to myself and more gentle in my approach is challenging, but not impossible. I have discovered by this mindset shift that I am calmer, more at peace, and filled with overflowing joy. Some say my spark is back, but I say I truly feel like I'm living again.

If you are anything like me, this lesson may be a difficult one. I feel it is actually one of the hardest lessons because it's extremely personal. I want to encourage you to take all the time you need before you proceed. As you think about all the things you need to forgive yourself for, invite God to sit with you. He already knows all, but having Him there will help give you the strength you need to forgive yourself.

The Unseen Truth

I realized how unkind I was towards myself with my negative thinking and self-talk. I felt God nudge me to change my ways and offer forgiveness to myself for the harm I had caused. This tough act brought a mindset shift so big, I went from a constant state of worry and anxiety to being calmer and more at peace, as joy filled my heart.

I had already forgiven others for things they said or did to me that caused harm. It was much easier than extending that same kindness towards myself. By finally forgiving myself after I let go of grudges and overcame regret, I no longer felt imprisoned. Perhaps now I can live life in a way that is far more enjoyable, as I give myself the freedom to laugh and have fun without criticizing myself for my actions.

Your mindset may not be the same as mine. You may still benefit from forgiving yourself for the times you were unkind in the past. I would love to challenge you every time you look at yourself in the mirror, to say one positive thing about your appearance. Leave the negative self-talk out, focus on encouraging yourself daily.

What is it you'd like to say to your younger self right now?

Braver with Belief

"'Come now, let us settle the matter,' says the LORD. 'Though your sins are like scarlet, they shall be as white as snow; though they are red as crimson, they shall be like wool.'"
Isaiah 1:18

In order to become braver with belief, we need to do some hard inner work by forgiving ourselves for being unkind. It is important that we silence our inner critic so we can amplify our inner cheerleader. It is far better to lift yourself up with positive thinking than it is to tear yourself down with negative thinking. God created you beautifully and with a purpose in mind. By being kinder to ourselves, we are honoring who God created us to be.

If you think about all the stress you carry from outside forces that amount to a lot of pressure—consider how much more pressure you are adding to that yourself. When you go to prayer and ask God to forgive you, remember He will wipe your sins away so they are as white as snow. However, if you continue on as you did before, you are continuing to sin. It's a vicious cycle that gets stuck in an infinite loop until you finally decide that you've had enough.

When we approach the topic of forgiveness, I like to start with seeking forgiveness from God in prayer, followed by forgiving others for anything they may have done that caused harm to me, and finally, forgiving myself for the part I played in contributing to my negativity.

This is the path to forgiveness that can help you become more resilient in your faith.

The Strength in Letting Go

I genuinely don't want to be miserable all the time, yet sometimes I can't help but scold myself for something I did or said that made me question it later. The enemy uses this weakness of mine as a pinch point to self-doubt so he can control my reaction. Realizing this tactic was being used against me helped me to stop from allowing it to happen altogether.

I had to stop the constant state of worry from filling me daily and change my vocabulary from *I can't* to *I will*. I had to be more confident in my daily interaction, and if I questioned why I said something, I had to remind myself that it was because it was the right thing to say in that instance. When you make this change, you'll notice that confidence returns and positivity becomes second nature.

It's time to let go of negative self-talk and work on becoming a more positive person. We focus so much on forgiving others, yet we rarely remember to extend forgiveness to ourselves. When we talk about overcoming regret, that regret can keep us fixated on the sin we've done. To overcome regret fully, you must also forgive yourself for holding onto it for so long. Recognize that you are human, and you make mistakes. And realize you are worthy of forgiveness, both from God and yourself.

Does it feel impossible to be optimistic? It can be easy to focus on the doom and gloom all around us and allow it to sway our outlook from one way to the other. Another trick I've learned is if I cannot control something like an unexpected circumstance—I have to be content with the outcome because I cannot alter it. Letting go of these things helps free up much needed brainpower to focus on the things you have control over and where you can make a big difference.

Moving Forward with Hope

Extending forgiveness towards yourself allows you the chance to be free from the shame and guilt you carry. Redemption is found with forgiveness. Once you have walked through forgiveness, do not dwell on it any longer. Let it go, so hope can fill its place as you mend past hurts. We'll cover this topic in the next chapter. Remember to check in with yourself often. Don't let the enemy distract you from God's calling on your life by trying to convince you that you aren't the right person to lead His flock. As you ask God for forgiveness of your wrongdoings, you should also extend forgiveness to yourself.

Braver Choices

Actionable steps you can take to become braver with belief as you step into the role of servant leader. I have broken it down for you in a way that is easier to remember: B.R.A.V.E.R.

Brighten: An action taking call to service to refine our hearts as we discover the area in which to serve.

Serving God: Write a letter to God, seeking forgiveness for the areas you are clinging to. As you write your letter, confess everything. After you finish writing, date the letter, fold it, and put it in your Bible to remind yourself later that God forgave you.

Reflect: A prayer that covers the emotions felt within each chapter with a promise to let go of the things we need to, so we can keep moving forward.

> *Father, I apologize for being unkind to myself. Help me let go of negative self-talk as I work on becoming a more positive person. Please forgive me for not being kinder to my temple. Amen.*

Act: An action taking exercise that forces us to get up and move forward.

Create a list of areas you feel you have wronged yourself. Examples include missed opportunities, negative self-talk, or poor decisions. Write next to each item a compassionate statement of forgiveness that begins with "I forgive myself for…"

Verse: Memorization of a Bible verse that helps us remember the lesson within the chapter.

Write the following scripture and post it somewhere you'll see it every day; maybe it's a bathroom mirror, refrigerator, or your home office. Memorize it and refer to it when you speak negatively towards yourself.

> *"Therefore, I tell you, her many sins have been forgiven—as her great love has shown. But whoever has been forgiven little loves little."*
> Luke 7:47

Explore: An action taking exercise to help us explore new possibilities we may not have yet thought of.

Spend time in nature, reflecting on the things you have been holding onto and how it feels now to be forgiven for those things. Offer a prayer of thanksgiving.

Renew: A journal prompt for us to reflect with God in solitude.

Journal Prompt: Write a letter to yourself, focusing on forgiving yourself for past mistakes and regrets. Honestly acknowledge the hurt and understand why you made the mistake. Express forgiveness to yourself.

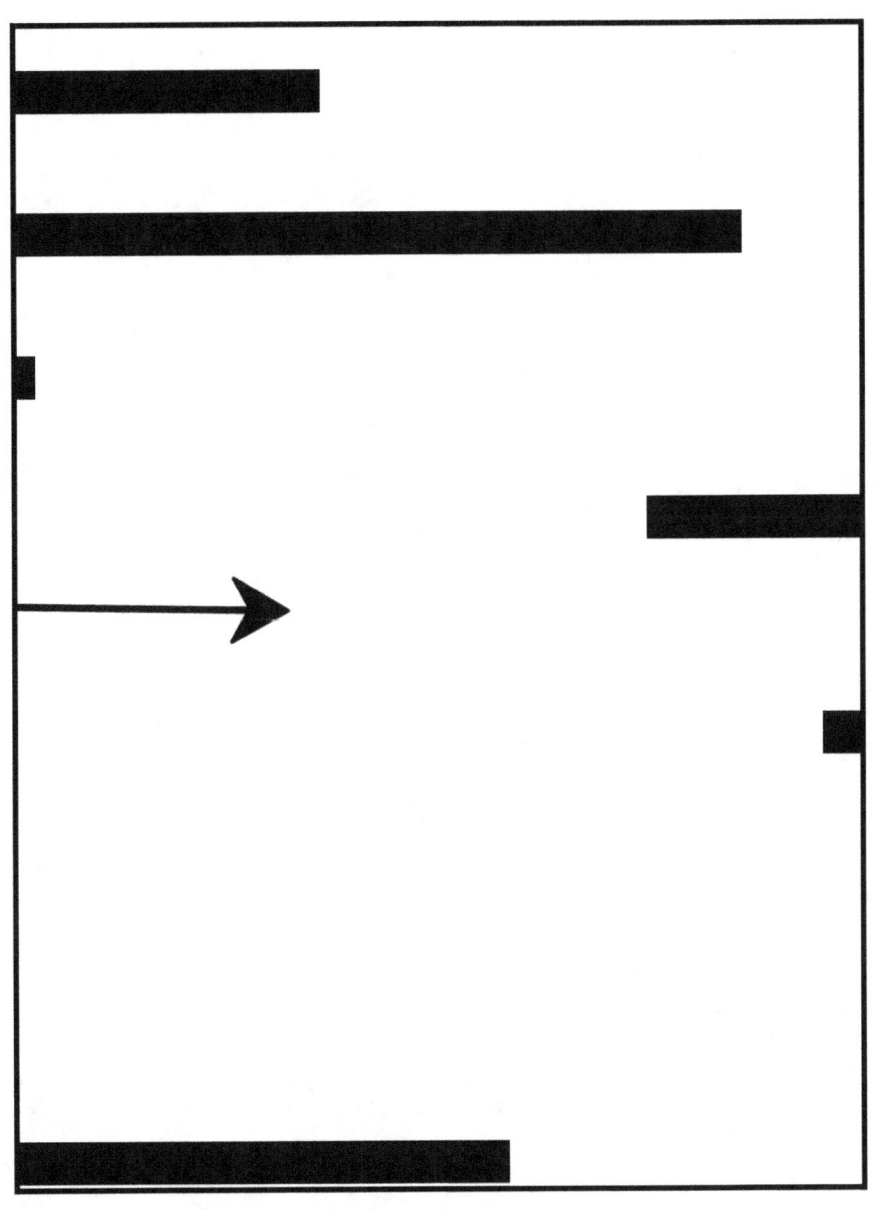

Chapter Five

Mending Past Hurts

Extending Forgiveness to myself was a new concept that, while freeing, brought to the surface a long list of past hurts that needed healing. The trauma I've endured in my life is something I quietly carried. I was unwilling to mend the pain because I thought I had to heal the source of the pain.

The more I tried to heal the source of the pain, the more stressed out I would get; I couldn't find a solution that cured what ailed me. This need to control and fix myself only slowed me down. I had to realize all on my own that without God, I wouldn't get anywhere.

Before we dive into this topic, I want to invite you to take a moment to relax your shoulders, release the grip on your jaw, and breathe in through your nose and out through your mouth. Did you feel a shift as soon as you did that?

January 2018 | Mended Spaces

Sometimes I catch myself tensing up: my jaw becomes clenched, my shoulders rise, and my neck aches. I carry most of my stress in my neck, and if I don't mindfully release it, a headache usually follows before the day ends.

Stress comes in various forms and for many reasons. Some reasons directly result from others, and some are there because we put them there. Over the years, I have become more and more stressed, which has caused long-lasting problems in my body.

When I was told I had to reduce my stress to help with my digestive issues, I started paying attention to what was causing stress to take root. What I uncovered surprised me, as I realized most of my stress was self-inflicted. Let's travel back in time so we can fully understand the root of my stress. We'll visit some things that significantly impacted my past, and I continued to carry them forward.

When Mike and I went through the fostering program many years ago, we transitioned three of our bedrooms into one nursery and two children's rooms while we waited on placement of children. The nursery genuinely excited me. Thoughts about the possibility of holding a newborn baby in the beautiful nursery brought me joy. However, as fate would have it, halfway through our training, we shifted the age to older children as we both felt the need to help there.

When our foster children moved in, they helped me transition the nursery into my office, where I could work from home while caring for them. Because I couldn't stand to work in a room that resembled a nursery, together, we covered the walls in a fresh coat of coral paint. That particular color turned out to be a terrible choice.

It was supposed to be a soft coral, pale and positive, but what I got was a bright, almost orange version of coral instead. There must have been an error in the mixing process at the store, because it didn't match the paint swatch I held in my hand. Every time I would go in that room, I could feel my stress level rising from the brightly colored walls. Yet, after the kids moved on from us, I couldn't bring myself to change the color right away because of the precious memories those walls held. I was overwhelmed by the disrupting color and filled with sadness at the memories around it.

One day, I came home after an extremely stressful day at my part-time job as an office manager, where I was wrestling with so many things. My own business was taking off, and the job I was working at wasn't fitting into the picture anymore. Facing pressure from opposing opinions on my career choice after my layoff, I was trying to fit in design work for a new client, while also maintaining my retail space at the local mall. I was juggling so many commitments, it was unsurprising when I dropped them all.

Feeling judged, misunderstood, and alone, mental exhaustion overwhelmed me as I struggled with the weight of it all. Coping with the loss of foster children and a miscarriage from the previous year was a heavy burden. It was a frigid January day filled with constant reminders of all I had lost. I shuddered in the cold as I wrapped my coat tightly around my shoulders before I headed inside my home after returning from work.

As I walked into my home office, I couldn't fight back the tears anymore. I collapsed into a giant, sobbing heap on the floor and wailed loudly as I asked God why this was the way my life was going. The pent-up emotions came flooding out as I could no longer stuff them back down and pretend everything was okay.

Grief has a way of coming out of left field and making it impossible to do anything but work through the emotions it brings. Alone in my house, I gave myself the freedom to release everything. Pounding the floor, I cried out to God, questioning His desertion. Blame fueled my need to scream at Him for how my life had become. Without holding back, I finally said everything I'd wanted to say about the situation—but never felt I could.

Eventually, I calmed down and felt bad for the terrible lashing I just gave God. I sought His forgiveness as I apologized for being too harsh in my delivery—yet still held firm in my belief that He contributed to the way things were, even if merely by allowing them to happen. My losses filled me with so much anger that I couldn't let go.

When I had cried the last tear I could muster, I looked around at my bright orange walls and I cringed. I decided then that it had to be a much calmer space to help reduce the amount of stress and anxiety the color was adding to me.

Changing the paint color was one thing in my life that I could control and shift the outcome. I got up off the floor, bundled up, and drove to the paint store. I looked at all the swatches for a color that filled me with a sense of calmness and decided on a very light neutral gray color. That weekend, Mike and I finished the room, and it felt like I could breathe again. I leaned against him, put my head on his shoulder, and thanked him for his help as I fought back the tears that filled my eyes. Letting go was difficult, but the relief I felt in that moment was like a weight lifting from my heart.

Shortly after my room remodel, I purchased a money tree to bring life into the space and give me something new to nurture. I named her Penny and I tend to and care for her daily, as I tell her good morning and check her leaves for signs of discoloration. I water her with bottled water because our tap water has salt in it from the water softener. This helps my plant thrive and continue to grow. Penny has become so big, she will need to be repotted in the spring into a bigger pot to accommodate her new size.

Caring for my plant has given me something tangible to do daily and aided in mending the past hurt of losing my children. It brings out my nurturing and caring side, along with my playful side, as I talk to her. It may feel silly to talk to a plant, but I talk to her in the same manner I talk to my pets, which has surprisingly helped me not feel so lonely.

The mere presence of life in the old nursery turned office helps bring a new energy into the space. Though these changes happened a few years ago, they have helped me enjoy stepping foot into my office every day to work. Rarely do I struggle with creativity block now, and I love how Penny creates the perfect backdrop for my videos.

You may wonder what this has to do with mending past hurts. I am an extremely sentimental person who has a difficult time letting go of things. I am afraid if I change something, I will forget the memories I was trying to preserve. By not removing the coral color from the walls, I was staying in place in my discontentment. Changing the color to a soft, soothing gray helped me relax and enjoy my space again. Once I let go of this need to stay frozen in place as a preservation, I discovered the change was extremely helpful in mending my broken heart.

Holding onto things or keeping yourself from updating paint on your walls keeps you focused on everything tied up within the space. For me, it was a reminder of never fulfilling my desire to hold a baby within those walls, and never again being able to hear the foster kids' laughter in the space. I knew I needed to mend my broken heart, but who I had become was different. I had to discover a way to mend my heart that fit who I was at that moment in time, and allowed for the greatest chance of healing to occur, with God at the forefront.

Mending Your Broken Heart

Recently, someone asked me how I have been able to heal past hurts in my life. I answered honestly by sharing I don't know if I will ever be able to fully heal those broken parts of me—but I have done my best to mend them in a way that helps me continue to move forward. God is the only one who can bring forth healing. But for areas in our lives meant to help us grow, mending is often the better solution. Healing is a full restoration back to the former self, whereas mending helps us to repair the hurt while creating a new sense of self.

There will always be something that reminds me of the pain I have endured during key moments in time. As each anniversary date draws near, I find I am filled with sadness as I remember. Sometimes I am so busy I don't even realize the date is coming up, but because our bodies have a way of remembering things before our mind does, there are always signs.

For me, it starts as added tension I carry in my shoulders and jaw, followed by an overwhelming sense of sadness that I cannot explain. Once I recognize this is taking place, I give myself the space to work with God through that sadness—and once I do that, I can get back on track.

The first few holidays after the loss of our foster children were the worst, as everything I pulled out reminded me of them. There were a couple of years I couldn't even put out the decorations because it was too painful. With time, I slowly reintroduced each decoration and put them in a different spot to create a new tradition.

Because the children are gone, the magic of the elf is gone with it, but Flake still appears and takes his spot resting on our mirror every year.

This year, I walked by and spotted him. It made me catch my breath and caused me to sit in the chair next to him as I allowed myself the space to work through the emotions as I remembered the children's time with us.

When someone is gone from your life, their memories may be all you have to remember them by. If you haven't been able to fully process your grief, the idea of mending your broken heart feels like a lofty goal. It's important to know we are all different in our grief timeline. Therefore, only you will know when you are ready to mend your broken heart. I caution you, however, not to let it consume you entirely and prevent you from enjoying the rest of your life.

Allow God the chance to restore your heart to help create the person you are in this season of life. Be careful to not seek healing in a way that removes or glosses over your experiences by obliterating them. The grief you feel is valid, and the memories tied to it are far too precious to wish them away. Truth is, you'll never be the person you were before you experienced grief, as it has forever changed you. And that is okay.

I don't cry as often when these moments come now. They absolutely get better as time progresses, and you adapt and grow as an individual. The same is true of grieving the loss of loved ones during holidays, as you carry on the traditions they've instilled in you since you were a child. You discover your new normal, despite the large void in the wake of their leaving.

You may be still learning what your new normal is now as you grieve. Please know there is no timeline with grief. Take all the time you need as those feelings come up. Work on mending those parts of you to help create resiliency in the emotional response. If you struggle with this, invite God to sit beside you as you process your emotions and ask for His help in mending your broken heart.

Draw Closer to God

There is nothing strong enough to keep us from the love of God. Remember this promise from Him as you navigate the grief you feel from your past hurts. It may feel as if He has left you during this time, when in truth, it is us who walk away from Him. As you stand, fixated in place, unsure of how you can begin mending the hurt you feel, glance behind you. It is there you'll see He is unchanging as He lovingly looks after you, with a longing to help you through your struggles.

The Bible recounts moments of divine healing, which is only possible through God. I have never witnessed the miracle of healing in my lifetime, but what I have experienced is a complete transformation of who I am. I can only attribute this to help from the Lord. The reason I can attribute it to God is that prior to it happening, I wandered alone in darkness as I walked farther and farther from Him.

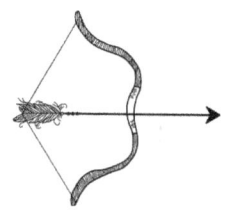

I didn't discover peace and joy until I returned to a life that put God first every single day.

Therefore, I have not only changed as a person, but my business has also changed. I feel strongly in my conviction that there is power in prayer and a relationship with God. I know God is my principal source of hope and happiness.

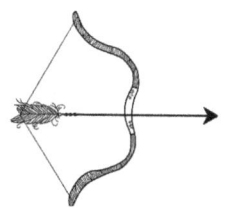

Life may still be difficult, but because I have done the hard work of mending my past hurts, I feel better equipped to face whatever comes my way with God by my side.

When I draw in closer to Him, I feel His presence move closer to me, which creates a new drive within me. On days when I skip spending time in conversation with God at the start of my day, I can see things slowly derail in front of me. Usually, this prompts me to stop what I'm doing and pray before doing anything else. My day may already be too far off the rails to bring it back on track, but at least now I feel like I can conquer anything.

The ways I intentionally invite God to join me throughout my day include prayer, study, conversation, and worship. I try to do these four things often throughout my day—not just when things are going wrong. Every time I take a break from work, I pick one of these activities to do. When I go on walks, I listen to worship music and sometimes sing along—which could likely be obnoxious to my neighbors if they are out! But I try to not let that stop me from doing it when I feel compelled to sing.

By allowing God to be more present in my life, He is helping restore who I am as my heart is refined. I know my heart doesn't look pristine and perfect; it has many jagged cuts that are now forged together by a single thread, woven in between by God. If you were to look at it closer, you may think it was the heart of someone who lived an unhappy life. A couple years ago, I would have agreed. Now I invite you to inspect it, while I point out the many repairs that have helped me become a better person.

I don't want my heart to be void of the growth I have encountered because of my past. When you look closer, you'll see how I have overcome it all. Because I am forever grateful for all God has done to see me through, I want to help others reach a similar place as I am now. It is possible for you to be here, too. With time, determination, and help from God, you can mend your broken heart.

Let it Out

Thinking back to the day I wailed on the floor of my coral-colored office, I see myself finally being able to let out emotions I kept pent up inside for a long time. I had gotten used to being strong as I carried grief on my shoulders and became void of emotions. It wasn't like me to hold it in like I had. In fact, that was the complete opposite of my characteristics.

When I felt sad, I would always spend time crying it out as I released the emotions, even if I didn't understand the origin. Over time, I ignored my feelings to dampen an emotional response, which only caused emotions to build up inside of me. As a result, my breakdown that day amidst the coral-colored paint showed me a need to listen to my body again and allow myself the chance to feel the emotions as they came. Being an emotionally in-tune individual gives you great insight, as it can show when you may deal with a potential problem.

With time and practice, I am now back to where I feel a healthy balance of emotions. I no longer suppress the desire to cry when I'm sad, and I also let tears fall when I'm filled with pride and happiness. It's who I am, and I'm okay with that. By allowing my emotions to occur naturally, I no longer have breakdowns like I did that day.

Don't be afraid to give yourself the freedom to process your emotions in a way that is comfortable for you. Find what works best for you and be sure to not suppress your emotions as they naturally arise. Learn to listen to your body. It has a way of telling you what it needs—and chances are if it is telling you to cry it out, you will probably feel better once you do. Invite God to sit with you as you process your emotions. There is no one greater who understands them than Him.

One thing I try to remind myself is that hurting people often hurt others. The way to stop this from happening is by becoming a healed person who helps others.

The Unseen Truth

I allowed myself the ability to let out the emotions that were bubbling up inside of me instead of holding them back. This natural release helped me to think more clearly towards a resolution that could help begin the mending process. This process looks different for everyone. Finding what works best for you will aid you as you begin to mend your past hurts.

Your past hurts have taken a piece of you away and created a lasting impression on you, shaping who you are today. By focusing on mending these parts, you are strengthening the weak point caused by the ripple effect of the hurt that was caused. This will give you the chance to become more resilient as you move forward and begin to lead others.

When remembering past hurts and feeling overwhelmed by emotions, allow yourself to feel them. Invite God to be with you as you safely release your emotions, and then look at the situation with a fresh perspective when you are finished.

What is something different you could do to mend your past hurts?

Braver with Belief

"'But I will restore you to health and heal your wounds,' declares the LORD, 'because you are called an outcast, Zion for whom no one cares.'"

Jeremiah 30:17

In order to become braver with belief, we have to allow God to help us mend our past hurts. Many times, as I worked through the grief I carried, I felt as if I were alone in what I was coping with and felt like an outcast among my peers. I kept these feelings bottled inside because I didn't want to dump my emotions on others.

One thing I now realize is, no one can fix the pain of the past that resides within my heart. I have received help through therapy and have confided in trusted friends—but even despite doing this, I still struggled to fully process my emotions. It wasn't until I invited God in and gave into the overwhelming emotions, allowing myself to sob without trying to restrict the sounds that came from within, I could move forward.

You are extremely brave for trying to carry it all on your shoulders, but even brave warriors need to release so they can relax. You cannot carry this much stress for long periods as it adversely affects your health and wellbeing. Always invite God to join you as you mend your past hurts.

The Strength in Letting Go

I have struggled with letting go of things that have hurt me in the past. One thing I try to remind myself is that it happened, and it is behind me. Memories don't have to be painful and can become something you look back on fondly, with a spirit of gratitude for all you've survived.

Visualize yourself walking on a tightrope where it swoops down and moves with every step forward as you wobble while trying to remain upright. This is how it is to move forward while carrying the stress of your past hurts on your shoulders. Once you mend the past hurt, you'll soon see that same tight rope becoming tighter and stronger and as you put one foot in front of the other, you'll make quick progress getting to your destination.

It is time to let go of the pain you carry from your past hurts. Pain is something we choose to carry long past the time we should. We forget we can let it go to proceed forward and allow mending to begin. The more you work on mending your past hurts, the less it hurts when you think about all you've lost. Because what happened was pivotal in making up who you are. We don't want to forget what has happened, but rather strengthen our response to the memory.

Do you feel you are suffocating under the weight of grief? We have been working on giving ourselves the chance to breathe again by working through some really difficult things; letting go of grudges, overcoming regret, forgiving yourself, and now mending your past hurts. It takes these steps to achieve a sense of peace that you have been missing for a long time now.

Moving Forward with Hope

Let's repeat the same exercise we started this chapter with. Relax your shoulders, release the grip on your jaw, and breathe in through your nose and out through your mouth. I want to challenge you to recognize the need to do this exercise during moments of stress. The more you do it, the more peace you allow to enter, which helps you move forward with hope—and without carrying the hurt you feel. Now that you have done the very hard work of helping yourself breathe again, it's time to learn self-compassion. I'll cover this in the next chapter.

Braver Choices

Actionable steps you can take to become braver with belief as you step into the role of servant leader. I have broken it down for you in a way that is easier to remember: B.R.A.V.E.R.

Brighten: An action taking call to service to refine our hearts as we discover the area in which to serve.

Serving Others: Reach out to someone you know who is currently hurting or grieving. Brighten their day.

Reflect: A prayer that covers the emotions felt within each chapter with a promise to let go of the things we need to, so we can keep moving forward.

> *Father, I am so sorry that I have been trying to carry the weight of my past hurts on my shoulders alone. Help me let go of the need to withstand the pain as I invite you to sit with me in my pain. Please forgive me for allowing this pain to cause additional stress in my life and not working towards mending it sooner. Amen.*

Act: An action taking exercise that forces us to get up and move forward.

Get a plant that can thrive indoors and is easy to take care of. Put it in a spot where you'll see it daily and engage with it every time you pass it. Touch it, name it, talk to it, and nurture it often.

Verse: Memorization of a Bible verse that helps us remember the lesson within the chapter.

Write the following scripture and post it somewhere you'll see it every day; a bathroom mirror, refrigerator, or your home office. Memorize it and refer to it when you feel the weight of grief causing you to confront past hurts.

> "*The LORD is close to the brokenhearted and saves those who are crushed in spirit.*"
>
> Psalm 34:18

Explore: An action taking exercise to help us explore new possibilities we may not have yet thought of.

Exercise: To mend your past hurts, you need to talk. Find a trusted friend or counselor whom you can confide in. Have an open conversation about the past hurts you are still processing. Process your emotions, gain a new perspective, and feel heard.

Renew: A journal prompt for us to reflect with God in solitude.

Journal Prompt: Write about the pain you're carrying. Focus on expressing how you feel with descriptive words. Write without judgment, allow yourself the chance to fully express every single emotion.

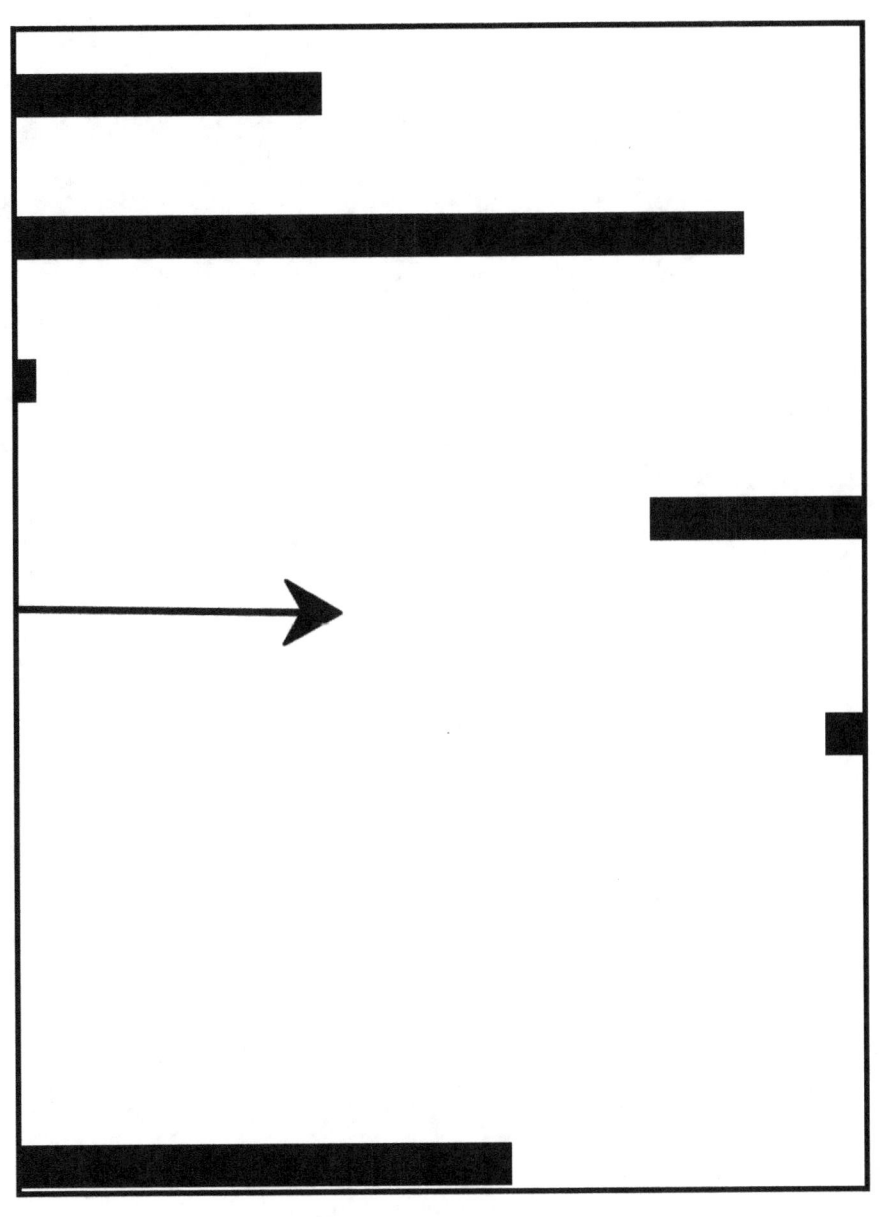

Chapter Six

Learning Self-Compassion

Surely by now, we are at a point where we've learned all we need to become braver with belief so we can boldly lead, right? Sorry friend, it's not that easy. We have only scratched the surface and still have a way to go. Stick with me in this. But first, let's look back at all you've accomplished up to this point.

You have been letting go of things that are holding you back from stepping into your God-given greatness. These distractions are obstacles placed in front of you by the enemy to keep you from going all in with God. The good news is, you are now aware of the devil's tactics, and are better equipped to handle what comes your way. It is important to keep going to ensure you are fully ready to shift into leadership.

As you work on mending your past hurts, you may find yourself more vulnerable than you'd like. This is when exercising self-compassion is more critical than ever before. But, if you aren't someone who naturally tends to yourself, where do you begin?

Self-Sabotage

It was one of those days when everything felt "off" and my mindset quickly took a nosedive into pessimistic territory. Everything I had touched didn't turn out like I had hoped, which delayed my progress and pushed back my deadlines. I dreaded the conversations I needed to have with my clients regarding this delay if I couldn't get it right. There was no time to waste on a break, and as I powered through lunch, I made progress on my project—though it simply wasn't up to my expectations.

My face flushed with heat as my body showed signs of food deprivation. Checking the clock, I realized it was time for my regularly scheduled afternoon break. To survive my demanding schedule, I decided food was essential to successfully navigate the rest of the day. While answering client project questions on my phone, I quickly reheated and ate leftover food.

As I swapped between phone and food, my leftovers grew cold during the extremely long conversation as I outlined changes needed for one of my projects. I scribbled notes in between bites because I didn't want to forget anything being discovered in the conversation.

Despite my best efforts, I was falling back into old patterns of putting the needs of others above my own needs because I didn't properly schedule the time it would take to do a far more demanding project than I was used to. I was teetering on the edge of burnout. I knew if I didn't get a handle on my schedule soon, my health would suffer. One of the complexities of having an autoimmune disease is that one small misstep could have a magnitude of consequences. If I got sick, it could keep me down for a long time—which would only make my already overbooked schedule worse.

The lack of food was creating the perfect storm inside my body; my mood had shifted into a raging beast. I felt like I was losing my mind with every text that came with yet another change to do from multiple clients—all at the same time. Normally, this wouldn't bother me because it is a natural part of the design process as my client discovers what they want the design to do in the end. But on that day, I was allowing my off-kilter schedule and clouded judgment to get the better of me.

I shoveled down the last bite of food, barely chewing before swallowing, causing me to cough as I choked it down. I fired off one more text as I looked at my reflection in the microwave door and shook my head at myself.

"*Why do you do that?*" I asked my reflection out loud.

The question caught my attention as I sat my phone down, stood there quietly, and looked myself in the eyes. What followed was a series of questions, as I asked myself why I thought it was a good idea to continue neglecting my body and health.

I stood there in silence for a moment as I tried to gather my thoughts. My instinct was to be critical in my answers as I imposed self-judgment for my shortcomings. I challenged myself, however, to take a different approach that was kinder, warmer, and more understanding of my situation.

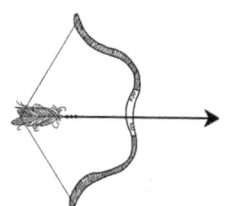

I reminded myself that we are all human, we all make mistakes, and we can all benefit from a little compassion.

Having already forgiven myself for being unkind in a way that contributed to my low self-esteem helped me to quickly work on not being a bully to my body and mind. Once I confronted myself and worked on changing how I respond negatively to a more positive approach, I started leaning into learning more about self-compassion and what the benefits could be for me.

The best way to test this was to put it into practice—and there was no better time than the present, where I felt I was being challenged. I put my phone on "do not disturb" as I spent some time in solitude with prayer and worship. Music has a way of changing my spirit. I worked through some breathing exercises to help calm my spirit, which also slowed down my increased heart rate. At that moment, I no longer felt like I was running a marathon, as I entered a conversation with God.

Feeling more like myself, I could get back to work and break through the barriers I had been facing earlier, which gave me confidence in the design I was producing. I finished the project I'd hoped to complete before day's end, and my client gave me feedback. I was delighted to discover I had captured her vision, and I officially completed the job.

Getting this project off of my docket was the goal I had set for that day, and accomplishing it brought much-needed relief.

That evening, I made a note to reevaluate my processes and procedures for design work for clients. I needed to determine if the time I was spending was being met with the proper payment or if I was selling myself short, contributing to my problems. Later that week, I performed my evaluation and found I had severely underestimated the time certain tasks realistically took.

Once I made this discovery, the next thing to do was the hard decision of a price increase to accommodate for the level of work I was doing. I wrestled with this choice because of my desire to help and please others. I would do anything to keep the costs low. However, I couldn't keep doing it to my own detriment. Ultimately, I realized that increasing prices and improving my scheduling were necessary.

Delays happen. And in this case, I had three clients who all delayed their project earlier in the year and came to me within days of one another to get back on track. Initially, I spread their bookings across my schedule, making it easy to manage each project's timeframe. With all three of them coming to me simultaneously, this was no longer the case.

Because I didn't want to say no to any of them, I overbooked myself—making it impossible to achieve what I needed in the time I initially promised. Rather than reschedule, I prioritized completing their projects at the expense of my well-being.

I recognized this as something I could not do any longer, as it contributes to major health concerns that will only grow worse with time.

If I want to serve others, I have to first help myself create an environment I can sustain long term.

I had to course-correct and work through my current situation the best I could so I wouldn't be completely overwhelmed again. Normally, I would have beaten myself up over this, but since I was trying really hard to be a better person, I told myself it would all be okay and work out in the end. Which is exactly what happened, despite working longer hours than I would have preferred.

Another Hard Lesson

The lesson I learned in this one extremely stressful week was that skipping meals is unkind to your body, depriving it of nutrients necessary to perform at its fullest function. While I am no health expert, I can assure you that I am a bear to be around when I'm hungry. The term "hangry" doesn't quite capture the shift in my tone that occurs as my blood sugar levels dip low from lack of proper fuel. Sometimes, I'm great at feeling it in time to fix the problem, but there are some days when it sneaks up on me and hits with a vengeance. I apologize in advance if you ever encounter me in this state. It's one I struggle to tame.

I also learned that when helping others, you cannot do it at your own expense as it will only exacerbate your stress levels. For instance, the beast that arises from skipping meals is often difficult to put back inside. The last thing I want to do is allow this to become something my client witnesses. Proper planning and meal prepping can really come in clutch, as it saves the day and keeps the beast at bay. It also keeps my mind sharp and helps me to focus on my work as I try to capture my client's vision.

Lastly, I learned that course correcting is a form of self-compassion that exudes kindness and love for oneself. The moment you realize something is going awry, take ownership and inform everyone it affects. I've had to eat my fair share of humble pie, as I had to admit my errors. Most people are understanding when things happen and prefer to be kept informed, rather than having details overlooked.

While these are issues I commonly struggle with, perhaps your situation is different. As you identify the areas you struggle the most and contribute to your stress, practicing self-compassion and kindness can help you completely shift your mindset.

By learning self-compassion, you can take even the most stressful of situations and rein it into a more manageable size. Be aware of your patterns in behavior as your stress level increases, and keep a log of trigger points. If you can identify the source of the stress, you may also determine the very thing needed to avoid it from occurring.

Learn to be mindful of your emotions. We discussed emotions in the last chapter, and I challenged you to allow your emotions to be processed as they come up naturally. Now we want to recognize the root of the shift of emotions as they occur, in order to determine the cause.

By learning your trigger points, you'll be better tuned in to how you can properly care for your body and reduce the number of reaction points; you'll decrease the amount of stress you are putting on yourself. It's easy to lay blame on everyone else for the stress within our lives, but we must acknowledge our part.

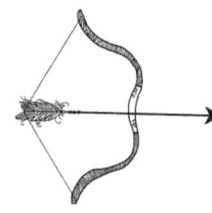 **Having clearly defined boundaries, especially within your career or business, helps reduce the amount of stress incurred.**

Other people may contribute to the stress you carry, but it is up to you whether or not to pick it up and carry it on your shoulders. Responding in a healthy manner will benefit you in the long run, rather than carrying the stress forward.

Becoming Self-Aware

Be mindful of old patterns that resurface when you least expect it. When we get comfortable, we sometimes let things fall back into patterns we vowed we'd let go of fully. You removed these patterns once to allow yourself the needed chance to grow. If you allow them back in, they quickly take root. And before you realize it, they have taken over again. If you find yourself in this situation, you have already advanced the battle by becoming self-aware.

To win the battle fully, however, becoming self-aware needs to be accompanied by taking action to course-correct the behavior you don't want to take root in your life. This takes time and continual improvement to keep it under control. Don't be hard on yourself if you struggle with this. It happens to all of us.

In Chapter Three, we talked about being kinder to ourselves. This is essential as you learn even more about what makes you do the things you do. Instead of beating yourself up about skipping a meal, find out why you skipped a meal, despite knowing the benefit of a consistent eating schedule. You may uncover a subconscious behavior pattern that contributed to your overall stress.

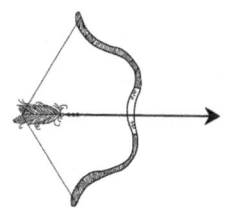

When things don't go as planned, practice responding in kindness and love instead of reacting harshly from a place of stress.

This has been difficult for me, because I often let stress control my actions and behaviors despite my best efforts. To combat this, I pause and redirect what I am currently working on when I feel my stress level rise.

Sometimes it's as simple as looking in the distance out the window to the tops of the trees. I watch as birds swiftly land on the tallest branches swaying in the wind. I allow my mind to wander about how God provides the birds with all they need and am reminded that He does the same for me. The shift in views is usually enough to pull me back into a kinder and gentler approach.

Give yourself extra time when scheduling things that come with deadlines. If you buffer in extra time when scheduling work, for example, you can relay a more realistic timeline to your client. This sets the expectation for project completion, and if something happens that sets you back, you'll have already worked in the extra time it took as a buffer. Ideally, the project will finish early without problems, benefiting everyone.

Each of these tactics works together to help manage stressful situations before they arise. It's not a foolproof combination, of course, as stress is one of those unpredictable circumstances that sometimes comes from left field. Therefore, understanding more about how you handle stressful situations helps you learn how to have more compassion not just for others involved, but for yourself as well.

Understanding Compassion

Understanding what self-compassion is helps you to determine if this is an area you need to improve. To be compassionate means you feel empathy or concern for someone else who is suffering or going through a hardship. Recognizing their need for support, you offer to help because you care. Apply the same approach you'd take helping others to yourself as well. You can achieve this by becoming aware of your pain and what alleviates it.

If I could sum this up into one act, it would be to become self-aware in all facets of your life. We can do this by paying attention to how we are responding, reacting, and feeling. It's important to notice these things during good times as well as high-stress situations to compare the two. I've learned during hardship, I have a tendency to check out as I disconnect from things that make me happy. Becoming self-aware of this tendency helps me identify when I disconnect so that I can stop myself from doing this. By learning more about my habits, patterns, and emotions, I can better handle them when they shift from one extreme to another.

This has helped me become a much better friend, as I have been able to control my emotions and allow myself the chance to actively listen and hear what the other person is saying. Because I can think much clearer, I am able to offer practical advice or solutions if my friend requests my help. By being more in tune with myself, I am also naturally happier, which means I can relax more around my friends as we have fun together and laugh so hard our bellies hurt.

When we feel good, we can do more of the things that make us happy. And I don't know about you, but I think laughing until my belly hurts is so much fun. It is something I have missed in my life and have been longing to get back. Spending time in fellowship with others always fills my heart with joy and gratitude.

Recently, I had friends over for a fun-filled evening where we celebrated the holidays, played games, and ate our favorite foods. Looking at all the delicious food, I had to exercise self-compassion, as I wished I could sample it all. However, I realized that eating something I shouldn't would make me sick for a week. I was kind to my body that evening as I filled my plate only with foods on my approved nutrition plan and refrained from indulging in holiday spirits.

Because my friends felt comfortable around me, they could eat and drink whatever they wanted and be themselves, despite my inability to do the same. As we all gathered around my table and played hysterical games, no one felt left out or out of place, and we laughed all night. The best part was because I didn't overindulge in something I shouldn't have, I could stay up well past midnight without feeling groggy or exhausted.

I am excited to say this is the first gathering I attended where I didn't over analyze everything I said or did that evening, as I was completely relaxed and authentic. It was an absolutely amazing night, and I hope my friends all felt the same way I did as the night ended.

What I learned from this approach is that when I give myself the chance to indulge in fun, my work with clients also becomes more fun. We are meant to have time to rest and rejuvenate.

Putting it into Practice

Perhaps you are still in a place where you are being hard on yourself for your shortcomings. Learning self-compassion helps us transition from being a bully towards ourselves to learning to love ourselves more like God loves us. In doing so, it creates a sense of love and fulfillment that brings joy back to our hearts.

Consider old patterns that could resurface in your life right now. Analyze them to uncover the driving factor behind the response and pay attention to the emotional response you have. If you discover trigger points that are easily corrected, like not skipping a meal, make scheduling your meals a priority to stay ahead of a potential stressor.

Keep a journal of things you discover about yourself that surprise you, or you haven't noticed before. Spend at least an entire week in observation when you detect a mood shift to collect valuable data about your habits and reactions. If you struggle to find anything, spend time in prayer and ask God to show you what you need to see so you can know yourself better.

It is in learning more about yourself, you'll be able to keep yourself in a better mental space to help others more.

The Unseen Truth

I fell back into old patterns by not prioritizing my needs in a way that helped my body, but hurt it. I now realize missing even one meal can significantly affect your mood and how you handle the rest of your day. Once I recognized what I was doing, it was important for me to self-correct and identify what caused this issue to happen.

How is your level of self-compassion? Is it something you practice regularly, or is that an area where you still struggle? It may be difficult to discern until a situation arises where it becomes more clear. Try to be more in tune with your mood shifts and determine the root cause of the pendulum swing from *everything is fine* to *now there is a problem*.

If you learn to have self-compassion when you are frustrated, it can help you have more great days and fewer bad days. Make sure you are meeting your basic daily needs instead of neglecting areas like skipping meals, drinking plenty of water, or getting enough sleep. Proper fueling and care of your body will allow it to perform at its peak, boosting overall productivity.

What is one area you can identify where you need to exercise more self-compassion?

Braver with Belief

"After all, no one ever hated their own body, but they feed and care for their body, just as Christ does the church."

Ephesians 5:29

In order to become braver with belief, we have to remember that taking care of our bodies just as Christ does the church is important. When we neglect basic care or needs, we risk crashing and burning in a way that has a ripple effect, affecting those around us.

I'm certain I am not the only one who has opted to skip a meal on a busy workday. Being kinder to myself when I miss a meal helps create a safer environment for me to want to choose healthier options. When I feel safe, I want to make the right choice by ensuring I eat my meals in a timely manner.

Properly feeding our bodies isn't the only form of self-compassion. Resting on days when you clearly need it, indulging in something that makes you happy, and spending time with loved ones are also ways you can show self-compassion as you recharge.

If you haven't become in tune with how your body responds when it is lacking something, I highly recommend keeping a journal of these things for a short time to help you identify the triggers and responses. This will help you make choices that honor your body and help keep you healthy and happy.

The Strength in Letting Go

Managing a consistent schedule, charging for the time it takes to do a task, and working in consistent meals on days when my schedule is hectic are all things that I struggle with. These struggles contribute to a shift in my mood from positive to negative fairly quickly. If I want to lead others towards a brighter future, leading in self-compassion will aid me along the way.

Because I don't want to risk my sour mood spilling over into the lives of my family, friends, or clients, it is important that I self-correct when these issues arise and learn how to avoid these triggers in the future. I used to wrestle with putting myself and my needs ahead of my desire to serve others. I had to remind myself that there is only one me, and if I go down because I couldn't take care of myself properly, then who would serve them?

It's time to fully let go of the negative self-talk and actions as you pick up affirming conversation. Understand the root cause and self-correct your behavior. Remember that properly feeding and caring for your body is honoring God as well. He lovingly created you and has given you this wonderful life to live. You can serve Him by making better, kinder choices for yourself.

When was the last time you skipped a meal to meet a deadline or because you were running late? My guess is it happens more than you care to admit, and before you know it, you may not have realized the problem in doing this. Perhaps it's not a meal that you are skipping, but sleep you've given up as you work late into the night. No matter what it is you are depriving yourself of, you could benefit from course-correcting and changing your schedule to allow yourself to care for your body first.

Moving Forward with Hope

God loves you for you. Instead of beating yourself up, extend self-compassion as you identify the problem and find a solution. Be kinder to yourself—not only physically—but within the thoughts you have surrounding your shortcomings. Know it is okay to reschedule where needed so you can have the time you need to be successful as you move forward with hope. A mindset shift, along with being present daily, is also crucial as we work towards being better, which is why I will cover these in the next chapter.

Braver Choices

Actionable steps you can take to become braver with belief as you step into the role of servant leader. I have broken it down for you in a way that is easier to remember: B.R.A.V.E.R.

Brighten: An action taking call to service to refine our hearts as we discover the area in which to serve.

Serving Yourself: Pick one thing that you love most that makes you feel great about yourself. Do that thing. Examples: Spa day, haircut, nap, cup of coffee, read a book, take a walk, etc.

Reflect: A prayer that covers the emotions felt within each chapter with a promise to let go of the things we need to, so we can keep moving forward.

> *Father, I am so sorry that I have neglected myself in a way that contributes to my overall stress. Help me let go of negative self-talk and actions while learning to pick up affirming conversation and prioritizing my needs. Please forgive me for allowing my negative mood to spill over into my daily interactions. Amen.*

Act: An action taking exercise that forces us to get up and move forward.

Mirror Exercise: Interview yourself to find out the root cause of why you are bullying your body and mind. Make sure you also forgive yourself at the end of this exercise, as learned in chapter four.

Verse: Memorization of a Bible verse that helps us remember the lesson within the chapter.

Write the following scripture and post it somewhere you'll see it every day; a bathroom mirror, refrigerator, or your home office. Memorize it and refer to it when you feel you are being too hard on yourself.

"The LORD appeared to us in the past, saying: 'I have loved you with an everlasting love; I have drawn you with unfailing kindness.'"
Jeremiah 31:3

Explore: An action taking exercise to help us explore new possibilities we may not have yet thought of.

Exercise: Take a walk outside if possible, and pay attention to how your body feels as you move and after you are finished moving.

Renew: A journal prompt for us to reflect with God in solitude.

Journal Prompt: Areas I can be more compassionate to myself and plans for improvement…

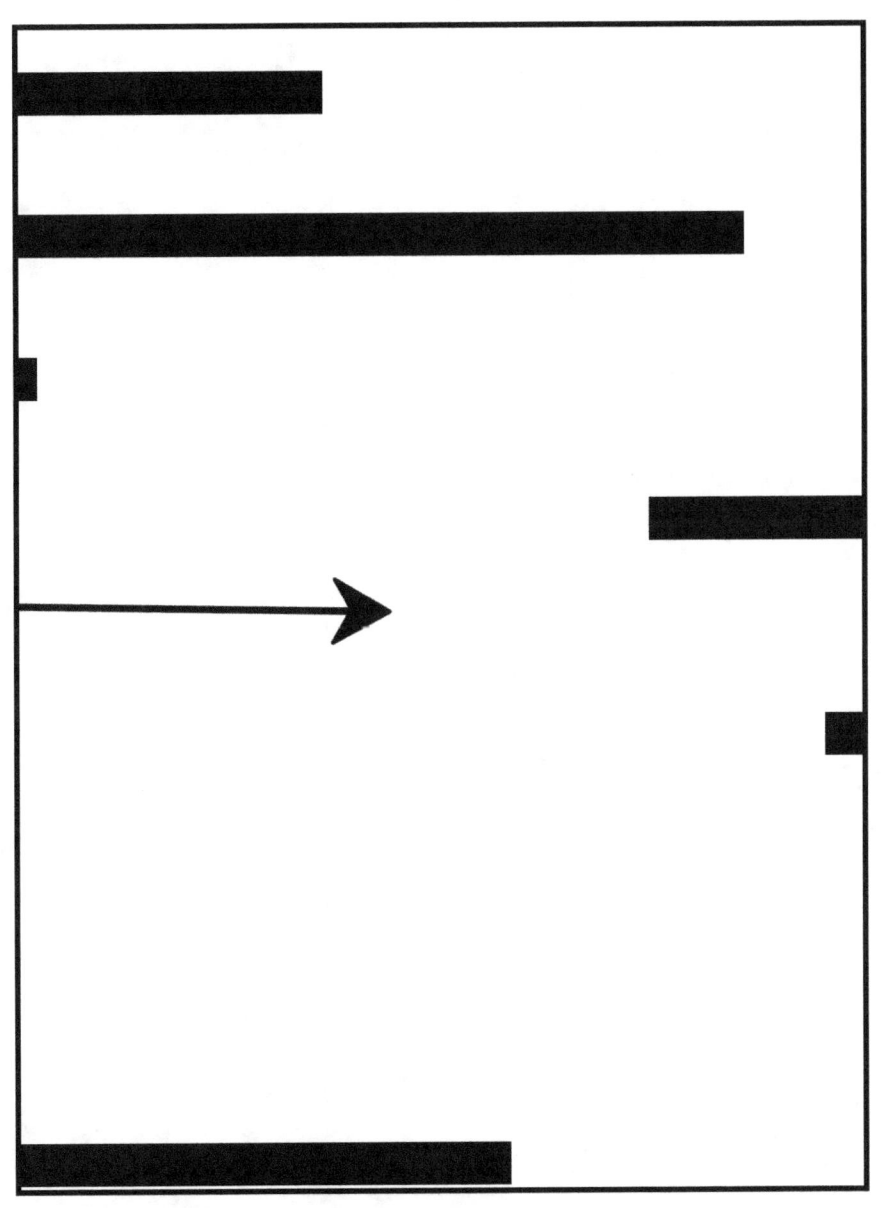

Chapter Seven

Mindset and Presence

Let me remind you of how far you've come. You have worked through unexpected circumstances, let go of grudges, overcome regret, forgave yourself, mended past hurts, and learned self-compassion. These lessons have opened your mind and helped you go from a negative standpoint to a positive one.

When we feel called to serve God, it is essential to protect our mindset, or we may doubt the validity of the calling. Every time I have had confirmation of my calling, I have denied myself the chance to progress forward with a plan to fulfill what God has lovingly placed on my heart for many years. This is primarily because of a negative mindset, where I believe I am unqualified to do what is being asked of me.

The truth, however, is that when I am obediently fulfilling the calling placed upon my heart, God is giving me everything I need to ensure my qualification to the calling. Because of this, all glory belongs to God for His goodness and provisions. God is able and desires to use anyone who serves with a willing heart—and He will always provide everything you need to walk in your calling.

December 2024 | Seek the Positive

Mindset can make or break any situation. The way you think and perceive things can control how you feel about a situation. To illustrate this point, I'll share a conversation I had earlier today with Mike, reflecting on how 2024 went for us.

I sat in the plush brown recliner with my laptop resting comfortably on its tray. As Mike walked by to let Coco outside, I paused from writing to stretch and check in with him. After closing the door, he walked over to where I sat and knelt down on the floor next to me, his hand resting inside of mine. These small moments of togetherness are something that helps both of us remain connected to each other.

We faced many unexpected challenges and setbacks in a tough year. Aside from having survived the tornado in May, we also battled damage to our house caused by flying squirrels taking up residence in our attic. The costs these new roommates caused us is one that neither of us were prepared to deal with, and required a great deal of repairs.

I suggested to him the result of this was a less than ideal year, but still a decent one. He challenged me by countering my disappointments with all the incredible moments 2024 brought. He reminded me it really was one of the best years we've had in a long time and reiterated that our house looked great with the new siding and soffits. He was absolutely correct. It really was an exceptional year. I learned in this conversation how much we both have grown. We talked about everything that transpired throughout the year and how we had so much to be thankful for.

We also discussed all the events of the year that caused the less-than-ideal situations. Although the campground tornado was not what we expected, the experience taught me a great deal. A pesky squirrel in our attic was also definitely not an ideal situation, but it helped us find other damage to our home that was in need of immediate attention. We can still use even less-than-ideal situations for the greater good. Find the silver lining!

As 2024 came to a close, I recall a day when I paused while scrolling on social media. Post after post filled my newsfeed with negative recollections of how terrible everyone's year must have gone. My heart goes out to those who had an awful experience. I've been there too. This was another reminder to always find the joy in every situation, no matter how dire it seemed.

I used to grumble when my year didn't go as planned. Especially if I failed to achieve my goals or faced some pretty awful trials. Eventually, I started using the very methods I had been teaching, and discovered that those years I thought were terrible—were actually great life lessons.

Long gone are the days of being driven by the dark cloud that hung over my head as my sour attitude threatened to ruin everyone's good day. I have done the work to become a person who chases joy daily, no matter the situation, and I am discovering peace instead of chaos.

By actively choosing to lead with a positive mindset, I remove negativity from my life, which naturally reduces my daily anxiety. I discovered this when I paid attention to how I reacted to things and kept a daily log for a few weeks. At first, I thought it was just a fluke to see a reduction in anxiety, and also wondered if it could have been in part to my diet change as well.

When I first removed everything from my diet to start with only twenty known and safe foods, I had a shift in my overall level of anxiety—but it didn't fully leave. I pinpointed the cause of my anxiety as an emotional response to the overwhelm associated with my schedule. I could test this theory by changing my schedule to allow more time in between projects, which ultimately proved I was correct.

By putting this fix into place, I was happier. And because I was happier, I was genuinely more positive. I would repeat this method of testing to uncover more areas in my life which were contributing to a negative mindset. And I found alternative solutions to correct this problem by going back through my notes when I was learning more about how I was reacting. I've discovered my increased positivity spreads joy to those around me, also improving their attitude.

My mood is often severely impacted by the people I surround myself with because I am very sensitive to their emotions. I never stopped to consider there could be others like me who have the same thing happen to them—and were affected with the energy I was putting off. This made me want to ensure when I was around others, I was careful to consider how my energy may affect them.

Mindset and Presence | 119

In the past, I have been told I was *a lot*. When you have big emotions and don't understand their triggers or how to properly express them socially, it can certainly seem overwhelming. I fully understand now what people meant by their statement of my "a lot-ness." I wish back then they would have taken time to explain the importance of understanding the reasoning behind my big emotions, and how to be authentically expressive without feeling overwhelming to others.

I've found that being a more positive person comes down to self-control. Another term for self-control may be willpower. And I always used to say I had great willpower when I was dieting because I could say no to dessert and be perfectly fine with that decision. If I were to exercise willpower with my overall mindset, I would actively choose the positive over the negative in every situation.

If I use my choice to eat foods on-plan instead of picking something off-plan to indulge in, the positive in this situation is I properly fueled my body. As a result, I feel amazing for the rest of the night and have a great time. The negative in this situation is I may miss out on the opportunity to eat something I once loved.

If I would have looked at this situation with the negative mindset, I guarantee you I wouldn't have had self-control, and would have devoured the entire package of caramel brownies—despite knowing I cannot eat gluten. As a result, I would be miserable for weeks as I made myself physically sick, which would negatively affect my overall mindset.

To best illustrate the power negativity has, I used this example because it shows a drastic result when we give in to the negative side of things. As we are focusing on moving forward and continuing to grow, leaning into the positive way of thinking will best help you accomplish this mindset shift.

As you serve others, you'll be able to help them find the positive within their situation by offering a different perspective for them to consider. Some situations may be more difficult to find silver linings, just as some individuals may not be receptive to hearing things positively when their world is falling apart. Don't let this stop you from being positive. There are plenty of people out there who need your help, and keeping a positive mindset will help you as you serve them.

Be More Present

There are many seasons in my life when I felt as if I was running completely on auto-pilot. Each day was filled with the same mundane tasks of waking up, eating, working, watching television, and going to sleep before doing it all again the next day. Sometimes, I catch this behavior quickly and am able to make the needed changes, whereas others take a bit more work on my part to identify.

Regret often accompanied the realization of the time that had passed during these days on auto-pilot. Because we know that letting go of regret helps free us, I desired to make a change in this area to avoid it from happening again. Once I identified my tendency to check-out during hardships, I began challenging myself to establish habits that not only helped me be more present in my daily life, but also contributed to having a more positive mindset.

With my positive mindset prepared, the only thing I still questioned was how would I keep up this new mindset and be more present daily? This is a place where you have to find what works for you because what works for me may or may not be it. I crave structure and organization, and I perform best when those things are in alignment. I have worked very hard on becoming an avid planner who sticks to the schedule as closely as I can, while still allowing room for things to move if needed.

I began working on developing healthier habits that promoted a positive mindset, like seeking joy in every situation, especially those where joy seemed to be missing. I also started practicing gratitude in my daily prayers because it was another piece of the puzzle I knew I was lacking in. On really tough days, I would take myself outside, sit and be still, and listen to the birds singing and the rustling of the leaves in the trees. These things helped me go from negative and angry all the time to more at peace and filled with joy.

I started new habits that aided my desire to be more present daily. Part of my coping mechanism has always been to pour myself into work to avoid the problems I faced. Because I desired to be a better person so I could better serve others, I knew I needed to approach things differently. I started strategically planning my days in a way that gave room for personal time, spiritual growth, work, and time with loved ones. I used a similar concept of a balanced plate to properly fuel my body by balancing my time in a way that was level and not tipped too fully in any one direction.

I accomplished this by using popular methods like time blocking, setting boundaries, time management, limiting my screen time, and using the powerful feature of the "do not disturb" setting on my devices. You may feel overwhelmed with all this information, especially if it is foreign to you—so let me break it down for you.

> **Time Blocking:** I started with my non-negotiable items and blocked out repeat time slots daily for things I wanted to make sure happened every day. Things like eating, sleeping, spiritual growth time, and time with loved ones.

> **Setting Boundaries:** This is always a difficult discussion to have with those we love and those we serve. However, it is imperative to keep things going smoothly. I let go of the constant need to respond immediately, and also stopped apologizing for a delayed response. I made sure everyone understood I would reply within the perimeters I set for each situation. I respond to clients during working hours only, family and friends as soon as I am free to do so, but with a promise to not allow more than twenty-four hours to pass.

Time Management: One of the hardest things you'll do is work on managing your time. You may need to audit your time to determine exactly where all your precious hours are being spent. Be honest—if you were scrolling on social media for three hours, that counts as three hours. Review your time spent and manage it in a way that honors God and honors what you are hoping to accomplish.

Limiting Screen Time: You'll likely discover the truth about how much time you spend on social media or browsing the internet during your time audit. Your results should lend way to a new schedule that limits your screen time to a more workable rate.

Do Not Disturb: Use this feature when you are working on something that requires your full attention. I use it during client meetings, client work, writing, and solitude. I have also started using it in the evenings by putting my devices to sleep so I can spend an hour before I go to bed doing something that helps my mind unwind. Usually this is reading or journaling, but any non-screen activity works best during this time.

Meal Planning: Every week, I spend one morning planning out my meals for the coming week. This helps me know what to expect for all three meals and one snack each day, which also keeps me on my plan with my maintenance protocol. After completing my meal plan, I immediately write my grocery list to ensure I have everything needed to follow my weekly meal plan. I also use the power of meal prepping where possible on grocery days to help reduce my time spent in the kitchen to open it up for more time spent with loved ones.

By strategically planning, you will create a structure you can follow as closely or loosely as you'd like. Leave room for things to move because life always throws us a curveball when we least expect it. By leaving room for things to move, you avoid adding extra stress to yourself for missing a deadline.

Perhaps it's my age or simply a preference, but paper planners and pens work best for me. My two-year experiment with digital planning showed it was easily forgotten, hindering my adherence to the schedule. While I do use digital planning to supplement my paper planner, my paper planner remains my primary planning tool. I check it first every day.

Find what works for you, as there is no one size fits most planner available. Work with your strengths and find one that fills the gaps in your weaknesses. They all offer significant benefits, and you can be as simple as you'd like or as detailed as you need to be. Find a planner that provides everything you need and that will point you in the right direction to get started with strategic planning.

Finding the Perfect Harmony

A few years ago, I had scheduled a fun September day mid-week to spend shopping with a family member an hour away. It was a day I looked forward to for many weeks leading up to it, having needed a break at the end of quarter three before jumping into an extremely busy retail season in quarter four. The day turned out to be lovely. We had such a great time we were both starting to get tired and decided it was time to head back.

We were fifteen minutes from reaching their house when I noticed my van began shaking and made a grinding noise when I turned the wheel. I had no idea what could be causing the issue because I had recently gotten new tires and had them aligned when put on the van.

When we got to their house, I called Mike to let him know the van wasn't safe to drive home.

This frustrated us both, but also provided a chance for us to work together to find a creative solution to a new challenge we faced together. He made the hour drive to get me and bring me back home where we devised a plan to tow the van on a rented flatbed trailer to our local mechanic. As fate would have it, the tie rod had fractured causing the van to be out of balance. We were incredibly lucky we found it when we did and took action right away to avoid a catastrophic tie rod failure. Discovering this was a moment of clarity for me about the importance of both alignment and balance simultaneously.

Each day still brings a new challenge, but because I am different—braver—I can accept each challenge as I optimistically work towards a resolution with God by my side. I can conquer the challenge by being myself and staying true to my beliefs. As a result, I feel accomplished and proud, not stressed or frightened. My daily movements have slowed to a more comfortable pace as I remove expectations and reduce the number of things I put on my plate. I am more in alignment with the woman God is calling me to be, as I have fully worked out the balance needed to keep me moving forward smoothly and confidently.

What could your life look like with more peace and balance? I would venture to say you would feel more accomplished, more fulfilled, and more loved. By being kinder to yourself and letting go of unrealistic expectations, you can create a more manageable schedule that works in the things you need to do and be more in alignment with God's will in your life.

You can't be in alignment if your balance is out of whack. Having your balance equally distributed keeps your life from going too far in one direction.

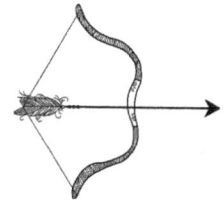

Once you regain your balance, alignment will easily follow, as both work together in perfect harmony to help you move forward and fulfill your purpose.

Mindset and Presence |

The combination of being balanced and aligned fills you with peace as joy returns once more.

There isn't anything you need to achieve this other than the determination to see a change occur within, and the bravery to take action and make it happen. You don't need any fancy gadgets or expensive tools; you can achieve this simply by reworking how you are spending your time every day.

As you plan out your new schedule, avoid putting unattainable expectations on yourself, hidden among the goals you set. Allow plenty of time for rest, relaxation, and relationships. We all need a little fun in our lives now and then, so be sure to leave room for opportunities that promote fun. Obviously, much of this will be affected by other factors such as your spouse, your kids, your job, or your business.

When you take your positive mindset and apply it to intentionally being present in your daily life, you'll soon fall into a new rhythm that feels more natural to you. If something within your schedule shifts your mindset to negative territory, consider looking for ways to remove it or create a shift to make it work better for you instead of against you.

Be sure also to keep some flexibility within your day, allowing for tender moments to be shared with your spouse or a friend. Work will always be there when you return, but time spent together is fleeting.

Pick one of these areas to start now. Focus on either transitioning your mindset to focus more on positivity as you get farther away from negative thinking, or begin rearranging your schedule to free up some time to be more present in your daily life. Once you complete one, move into the next one immediately after. Balance and alignment work well together. You will find you'll quickly fall into alignment once you've mastered balancing all of this.

The Unseen Truth

I realized the need to work on a positive mindset and become more present in my daily life. I wanted to stop coping by pouring myself into work and start living by inviting time for connection with those I love.

Finding the perfect balance in my schedule was crucial for me to achieve both of these things.

What does your schedule look like? Does it give you room to enjoy time doing things you like doing with those you love, or is it causing more stress? You can achieve the right balance by doing a time audit and determining where you spend your time each day. Be honest with yourself during the process. It is extremely important for the accuracy of the audit.

If you haven't yet been able to shift your mindset fully from being negative to positive, I want to encourage you to seek joy in every situation. Yes, this means even the hard ones that feel as if there simply cannot be a single ounce of joy within. Look closer—you'll find it.

What is one change you can make today that helps shift your mindset and will aid you in being more present in your daily life?

Braver with Belief

"Finally, brothers and sisters, whatever is true, whatever is noble, whatever is right, whatever is pure, whatever is lovely, whatever is admirable—if anything is excellent or praiseworthy—think about such things."

Philippians 4:8

In order to become braver with belief, we need to shift our thinking to focus on more positive things. This is an act that many people say is extremely powerful and absolutely will work—but it also takes a level of self-discipline that most will quit before they achieve what they hope to. Nothing good is ever easy. It takes hard work to improve habits that you have had for a very long time. Don't give up on yourself; keep persevering to achieve a more positive mindset.

In the same way that you are working on improving your mindset, choosing to work on becoming more present in your daily life will help you bring peace back into your life. When we go through hardships or unexpected circumstances, we may find ourselves in a state of survival. Usually, the first thing to go is planning out our daily interactions. By strategically aligning your day in a way that accomplishes everything you hope to achieve, you'll end each day happier and more fulfilled.

Take time to determine how you would like to spend your days. After you do your time audit, compare it to your goals and determine if they are in alignment or if they are off-balance. Make adjustments to create a balanced schedule that works with you and not against you. Leave room for things to shift, as delays often arise and are out of our control. Let go of responding in anger when changes occur, and do your best to respond with love and kindness.

The Strength in Letting Go

When I worked on healthier new habits, I would get frustrated with myself when I struggled in the beginning. While it's okay to feel frustrated, I want to be careful about responding negatively to a particular situation. In the past, I would give up quickly if things didn't go my way and caused frustration. This was only contributing to my overwhelming sense of failure and has now confirmed the need to dig deeper and try harder.

I failed because I was not using methods or tools that were right for me. I had to figure out how I could be successful and what products would help me achieve my desired outcome. Additionally, I had to work on changing my mindset to be more positive.

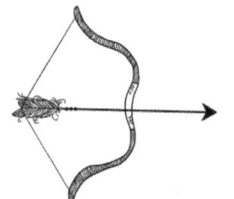 **Focusing on the true, noble, right, pure, lovely, and admirable things keeps us on target.**

Being present in today instead of worrying about tomorrow will help keep us on track daily. Managing time spent on things outside of these parameters will also help free up time we've lost along the way, allowing more freedom to do the things we feel called to do.

It's time to let go of the negativity and shift into a more positive lifestyle by forming new habits. Give yourself permission to slow down in your approach as you make these changes—and don't be hard on yourself if you mess up. Becoming more present in your daily life means intentionally engaging with others around you, learning more about what you like or don't like, and finding what works for you beyond just finding a planner.

When was the last time you strategically planned your schedule in a way that was balanced? Stop rushing to keep the peace, and consider how more balanced planning will help you in the long run.

Moving Forward with Hope

We are all given the same twenty-four hours in a day. How we choose to spend them is entirely up to us. How much of the time spent is in alignment with God's will for your life? By focusing on strategic planning with a positive mindset, you can bring balance back to your schedule and find time to spend it in conversation with God daily as you move forward with hope. Change can be scary and another added level of stress that is difficult to overcome. We'll discuss this in the next chapter.

Braver Choices

Actionable steps you can take to become braver with belief as you step into the role of servant leader. I have broken it down for you in a way that is easier to remember: B.R.A.V.E.R.

Brighten: An action taking call to service to refine our hearts as we discover the area in which to serve.

Serving Others: Instead of spending an hour watching TV, spend that time having a conversation with a friend or family member you haven't spoken to in a while.

Reflect: A prayer that covers the emotions felt within each chapter with a promise to let go of the things we need to, so we can keep moving forward.

Father, I am so sorry that I have maintained an unbalanced schedule and neglected time spent with you. Help me let go of becoming negative when there are delays and shifts in my schedule, causing the need for a pivot that may leave me feeling more stressed. Please forgive me for allowing my time to be spent on things that do not matter. I promise to rectify this by scheduling more time on the things that are pleasing to you. Amen.

Act: An action taking exercise that forces us to get up and move forward.

Meal plan for the next week. Think through each of your three meals and choose items that help create a well-balanced plate. Write up what you will eat for all three meals for seven days and create a grocery list for the items needed to create those meals. This will help you out when it comes time to go get groceries and you'll already know what to expect for meals. Take it a step further by meal prepping what you can once you get the groceries to help save on time spent cooking.

Verse: Memorization of a Bible verse that helps us remember the lesson within the chapter.

Write the following scripture and post it somewhere you'll see it every day; a bathroom mirror, refrigerator, or your home office. Memorize it and refer to it when you feel you are unable to be present like you'd like.

"There is a time for everything, and a season for every activity under the heavens."

Ecclesiastes 3:1

Explore: An action taking exercise to help us explore new possibilities we may not have yet thought of.

Exercise: Start your day with a mindset affirmation. Starting your day in a positive mindset will help you as stressors come up. Repeat the affirmation when challenges test your optimism.

Affirmation: I trust that God has good plans for me today, and I will walk in His purpose with joy.

Renew: A journal prompt for us to reflect with God in solitude.

Journal Prompt: Where in my hectic schedule can I carve out time weekly to devote to planning consistently?

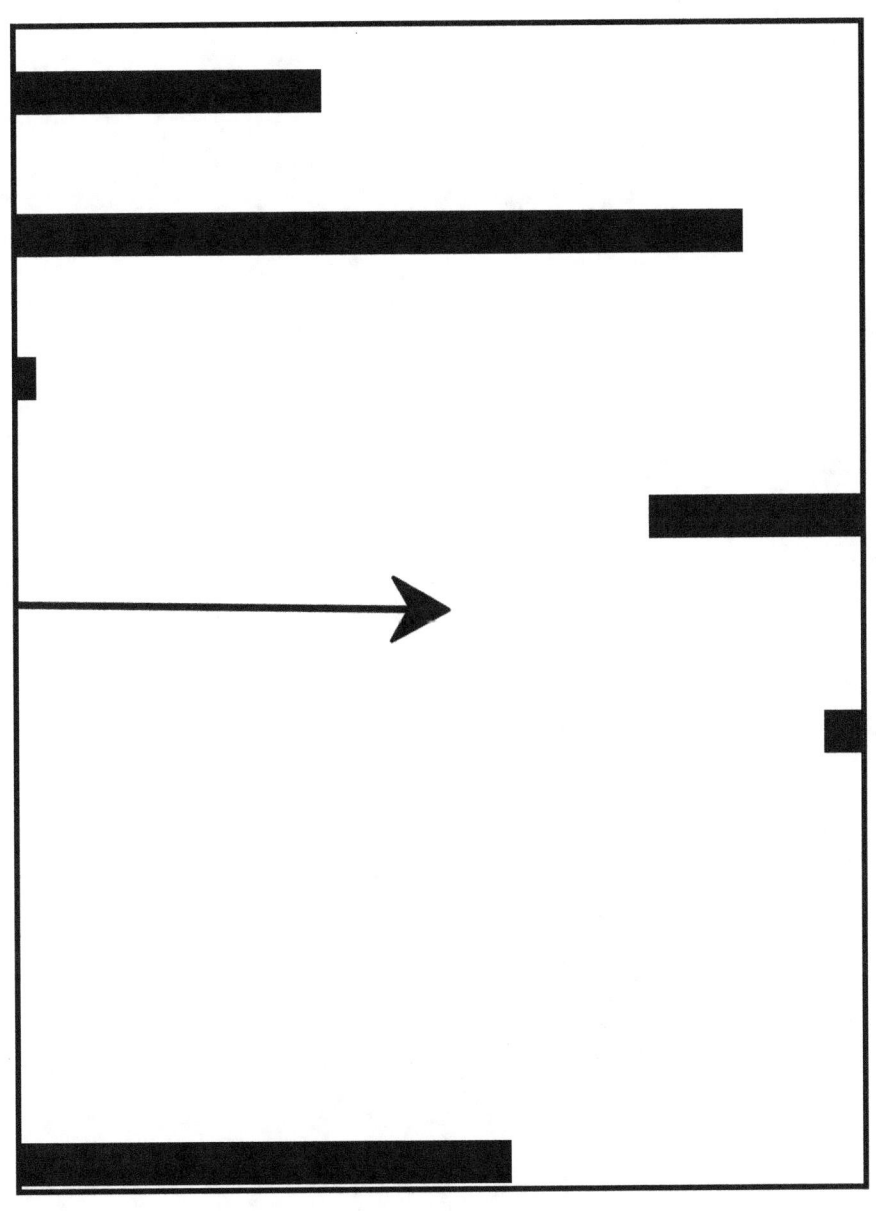

Chapter Eight

Don't Fear Change

With a positive mindset, it feels as if you can accomplish anything you set out to do—and more. The question remains, however: are you willing to change to become the woman God created you to be?

As I wrote that question, I had to sit with it for a moment before moving forward with writing this chapter. Conviction is placed in your heart by the Holy Spirit to gently and lovingly guide you towards repentance, growth, and freedom. Its counterpart, condemnation, is a tactic the enemy uses to guilt you for your shortcomings and keep you in a place of unworthiness and fear.

Confusion may arise when you try to discern whether you are facing conviction or condemnation. Because the more the Holy Spirit convicts you, the more aggressively the enemy will try to condemn you. As you are pulled back and forth between the two, anxiety often bubbles up inside and your judgment may become clouded. The only way to stop this from happening is to change your approach in handling the situation.

October 2017 | Forced Change

My heart raced as I quickly turned around to rush back to my oversized desk at the front of the building. I had clearly walked in on a meeting I shouldn't have—and discovered the rumors were true and layoffs were happening.

At the front of the building, I was greeted by sunlight pouring in from the windows, casting its warm rays across my desk. As I sat down at my desk, I looked around at everything in my area to etch it forever in memory. Dread crept up, and I had a terrible feeling I would be called into that room to learn my fate soon. I hoped I was wrong, because working at this company was something I loved. I hoped to retire here.

My phone rang and as I saw the words "Conference Room" flash across the screen, my heart sank. The caller instructed me to come in for a meeting. After I hung up, my feet refused to listen to my commands to move. I stood there, taking one last look before I made my way back down the long dark hall to the conference room. I took the empty seat closest to the door, emotionless, as I already knew what was to come next.

I remember little of what they told me in the conference room, because I was only thinking about the one person missing from the meeting. She should have been there when they told me I was being let go because of cutbacks. After they dismissed me to gather my things, I glanced into her office as I passed—and she avoided looking at me. I don't know what hurt more, her prior assurances that my position would be safe, or her lack of attendance in the meeting.

Because of my role within the company, I had a feeling cutbacks could happen; I had been noticing common indicators. As a precaution, weeks before, I began slowly removing accumulated belongings from my workspace to reduce the number of items I had there. Things like coffee mugs and mug warmers gifted to me from a friend, excess snacks, and drink mixes I had brought in to have on hand.

It didn't take me long at all to pack up what few things I had remaining. To avoid hearing others meet the same fate as me, I decided I would never walk down that hallway again. I escaped out of the front door to walk the block around the back of the building to get my van.

In front of the building, I pulled into a parking spot, went inside to quickly gather my belongings, and left quietly. Wondering what I would do next, I cried the entire drive home. Finding work had always been challenging for me, despite my experience. I knew I was incredibly fortunate to have gotten this position, because most companies now require a college degree, something I lacked.

This job was special to me. It was the first job I had after the foster children left and I ventured back into my career. During my time spent at this job, I learned several new valuable skills I wouldn't have otherwise learned. My job was a mix of responsibilities ranging from assistant, accounting, Human Resources, office management, and marketing. I was grateful for the opportunity to design the company website and marketing materials, showcasing my design skills, and assembling the clients' Christmas gifts was a yearly highlight.

I worked directly with the owner of the company, and I really looked up to her for all she taught me. She saw my potential and gave me hope. My confidence was boosted as I had the opportunity to showcase my skills. I was leaving her company with more skills than I had when I first started. I just wish I would have gotten the chance to thank her for giving me an opportunity for as long as she could.

My arrival home left me devastated, terrified, and unsure of what to do next. Looking back, I realize this was another necessary change in my life for me to be willing to fulfill the calling God placed on my heart.

2017 was one of the hardest years of my life. Considerable changes within my world that were beyond my control took place—and I hated it. I felt as if I was a passenger in an erratically moving vehicle as it careened out of control, headed straight towards a cliff.

In March, I had a miscarriage. The miscarriage reopened old wounds surrounding my infertility, despite accepting that I would never be a mother. Right before my miscarriage, I had finally reached a point where I was enjoying life again after losing our foster children. I had done my best to make it through and come out on top. But after the miscarriage, I found myself at the bottom of the ocean, feeling as if I was drowning.

In early October, another change came. On Halloween, I had scheduled a procedure to be done to remove a spot on my chest, due to a positive result for Basal Cell Carcinoma. This wasn't my first positive diagnosis, but it prompted a change in my products and a warning to minimize sun exposure. The procedure left a giant scar that is still visible today. I found myself trying to hide it, despite the difficulty in doing so. This change in my appearance added a whole new slew of insecurities.

And then a few short days before my scheduled cancer removal appointment, on October twenty-sixth, I lost a job I loved along with the confidence it had brought me. This third major change within the same year forced a life change I wasn't ready for, as I was still coping with the first two. To say fear settled in would be an understatement. It gripped hold of me so tightly, I was completely overwhelmed.

The grip tightened around me, squeezing out every ounce of will to fight I had as I wrestled against the way fear trapped me in place. The more I tried to break free, the harder it became to get a hold of the situation I found myself in. My future was unknown, and that scared me more than anything.

Have you ever felt like this? I could never sit back idly while my world changed around me. I would do whatever I could to fix—or even try to control—the situation to have a more desirable outcome.

Overcoming Fear

I no longer had a guarantee of steady income, and my future looked uncertain. My frustration stemmed from similar experiences at nearly every previous job that ended in layoff. I worried about how this job's ending would affect my long employment history. Despite my desire for longevity with a company, I had worked myself into a career that seemed disposable. The over-saturation of administrative workers meant employers had a wide net to cast, as they hired someone with less expensive salary requirements.

With no time to waste, I immediately updated my resume and began applying for open positions I found online. I spent the next couple of months applying, scheduling interviews, and typing up cover letters on a rinse and repeat schedule. I grew concerned I would never find work within the career I felt would be sustainable through retirement. Because of timing, the job pool was incredibly scarce as we approached the end of the year, making it difficult to find many opportunities that were a good fit.

In between job interviews and rejection letters, I wrestled with an overwhelming sense of fear and even began to question my capabilities. I heard the same responses over and over. My lack of a degree or over-qualification led to rejection. After a lengthy discussion with Mike, we agreed it would be a good time for me to consider doing something I always wanted to do. His support, encouragement, and belief in me gave me the confidence I needed to believe in myself again.

I pushed fear aside to focus on learning new skills and launched my stationery business while still applying for jobs. For a long time, I really wanted to design, develop, and sell my own products in retail stores—but I was unsure how to start. But that didn't stop me from doing all I could to make it happen.

My job taught me the skills I needed to build a solid foundation for my business. Having had a lengthy career writing Standard Operating Procedures and Operation Manuals, I started with writing SOPs for my business. If I was unsure of a step or resource needed, I researched it before proceeding—because I knew having a solid foundation would give me the best chance at long-term success. The more I built, the less scared I became; the possibilities before me were exciting.

With a fully organized list of instructions, I could begin developing my product lineup. Once I designed the products, they were moved into operations where I printed, assembled, packaged, and priced them. Finally, it was up to me to find the places where I would sell them. I sold products on my own through a website I designed and built. I attended vendor events and shows and eventually the door opened up for me to enter a retail space to see my dream come true.

A mixture of excitement and determination flooded my heart. Things moved very quickly once I began building out my retail space. The one thing I will never forget, is the feeling of pride and accomplishment I had when I stood in my space on opening day.

Imagine if I hadn't overcome the fear of never finding work again. I could very well have continued on my fruitless search for a job—or worse yet, landed a job I was miserable in. By overcoming this fear and taking matters into my own hands, I have successfully owned and managed my own business since 2017.

Buckle Up

We may dread and fear change because we do not know what will come next. When we look at what lies before us and it looks dire compared to how it used to be, it's natural to have an overwhelming sense of fear. The choice to start my own business or continue seeking a career was a pivotal moment that could severely alter the rest of my life, and I could only hope I made the right decision.

There were plenty of naysayers when I made the decision to start a business—I even lost friends. Looking back, I view this as God clearing the path to open my life up for an incredible opportunity; one that has undoubtedly changed my life. The most amazing thing to come out of this change? My skill set has more than doubled from the time I first lost my job to where I am now. Should I desire to return to corporate work, I now have far more I can offer an employer.

What chasing my dreams taught me is that you will always have the chance to make a bold change in your life. I understood that my career isn't my calling, and sometimes taking a giant leap of faith is needed to get back on track.

I could have painstakingly sat and waited through rejection after rejection. To survive the financial shift, I briefly accepted a part-time job before my business began to grow. Eventually, however, it became extremely difficult for me to uphold the work requirements of the job along with the demands my business garnered.

This resulted in another change in 2018, where I accepted my first freelance graphic designer role and walked away from the part-time job I was working. The decision to go full-time with my business was absolutely the best decision I could have ever made, and it has proven to be the case ever since.

I did not know if adding freelance work to my product lineup was good enough to work or if I would wind up flat on my face. However, I had the desire and drive to try my hardest to make it work. When you face a change this big—where your future depends on the outcome—how do you decide what is best for you to do? I would typically let my instincts take over as I did all I could to survive the shift. In doing so, however, I missed out on the greatest chances I had to make a change for the betterment of my life.

Is the fear of change keeping you from discovering what you need to do in order to fulfill your purpose? I completely understand how terrifying it is to take a giant leap without a safety net underneath to catch you should you fall.

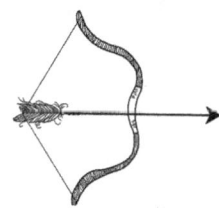

I may still fall flat on my face from time to time, but what I have found is the more I step out in faith, the more God shows me where His hand is my safety net.

Because God is never-changing, He is the one constant as your world shifts and bends to become something different. How you approach a season of change will be the deciding factor in how you survive the change. Things simply do not fall in your lap as if you've hit some imaginary lottery. The direction you take your life in directly results from the actions you took to steer it there. If you continue to sit frozen in fear, so there your life remains.

Others cannot change your course, despite their power to influence your decisions. As you receive guidance from others, it is up to you to determine if the choice you make is the correct one, as you alone may suffer the consequences of choosing incorrectly. Taking charge of your future begins and ends with you grasping hold of it and trusting God to help you keep it straight as you press onward. Buckle up, friend. It might be a bumpy ride.

With big changes, grief can also accompany the sudden loss and shift in direction. We rarely talk about the grief associated with losing things other than people. I've observed myself and my friends struggling with grief from losing jobs, businesses closing, moving to unfamiliar places, and accepting the impossibility of deeply desired things, like children. When faced with a major change, it is important to take time and process the emotions and feelings that come with it—with God by your side.

New Chances

Whether you are currently facing a major change or one is just around the corner, remember: no matter what lies ahead, you can use all you have learned to propel you forward into your next chapter. Don't be afraid of change. Because sometimes, change is actually something that works out far better than we could have ever imagined.

The old, more negative version of you may see change as something to dread and fear. Aren't you grateful the new, more positive version of you can view this as a new beginning? Let your imagination run wild as you consider all the unique possibilities that await you now. If you could do things differently than you have in the past, I would encourage you to make decisions that are authentic to who you are.

If you could choose the area in which you will lead, what would it be? If God has placed a calling upon your heart that you haven't yet been able to cultivate, maybe now is the time. The more you release what holds you back, the more space you are freeing up to begin working towards fulfilling your calling.

As you decipher where to go or what to do, resist the urge to seek advice from outsiders who may be unsupportive of your goals. If you have trusted friends to discuss your situation, view their advice as the data required to come to your own conclusion successfully. Understand that their opinions are merely data—not the force guiding your direction. Only one person knows the answer. And if you aren't actively seeking Him, you may continue to get lost along the way.

Many times, I, too, have sought advice from friends and wound up even more confused. Though it would make them happy, settling for something that pulled me from my purpose would have made me miserable. Their advice became valuable data that helped me weigh the pros and cons of my situation. Their wisdom in my situation from an outside perspective was timely in what I needed to hear to dig deeper into my discovery with God.

In my experience, friends and family were not mad if I did or didn't do what they suggested, as they happily supported me in all of my endeavors. I found that choosing what made me happiest freed up my time to spend with them in fellowship, rather than seeking approval.

If family or friends judge your decisions harshly, it is acceptable to lovingly remind them you may live your life as you choose. That is the beauty of being an adult. We get to decide what we do and don't do. We know what is best for our lives better than anyone else because we are the one living it, and we are the ones who will face God on redemption day. Don't make your life harder on yourself by being someone who is driven only by pleasing others instead of pleasing God.

The next change you face, I pray you face it with a renewed sense of confidence. Know it won't be easy, but that it's okay to continue moving forward with God leading you. Look forward to the new opportunity that awaits you, with all the fun discoveries change promises to bring.

The Unseen Truth

I had to accept that I wouldn't go back to work in the traditional sense. Change showed me it could be less scary. I could use everything I had learned, which meant I wouldn't lose all the things that I had worked so hard to build. To succeed in my new business venture, I knew I would need to work extremely hard to establish and maintain it properly. It's hard to believe that soon, I'll be celebrating my ninth year in business as I scale it in a way that continues to fulfill my calling.

What new opportunity can you discover within the change you now face? It's difficult to see the potential before you if your situation seems frightening. But when you consider all the skills you have acquired and how you can use them now, you may discover the answer you seek.

If you haven't quite conquered the fear of change, don't lose heart. I encourage you to take time and consider how you can use this situation to better your overall positioning. By assessing the situation you are in and taking action to improve it, you will get back on track.

What change are you facing right now and how can you put your hope in God as you face it?

Braver with Belief

> *"For I know the plans I have for you,' declares the LORD, 'plans to prosper you and not harm you, plans to give you hope and a future.'"*
> Jeremiah 29:11

In order to become braver with belief, we have to remember God knows what our future holds. We can have hope no matter what happens now. With God on our side, we can look forward with hope for a brighter future. Remember, fear is a tactic the enemy uses to keep you from fulfilling your purpose. Move beyond fear into a more hopeful place as you go forward in a new direction in leadership.

Give yourself the time you need to process everything happening all around you. With some changes, grief may also accompany fear. Listen to your body as it responds to everything you are going through and take the time you need before moving forward. Trust your judgment and seek the Lord first before seeking advice from others.

If your emotions are controlling your actions, take time to process how you are feeling, and spend time in solitude. Keep in mind that during solitude, the goal is to have conversations with God and invite Him to be a part of your life and decisions. Be honest and open to how you are feeling at this very moment. Give it all to Him.

The Strength in Letting Go

With change, being brave is not something I default to. I am a creature of habit who looks forward to a meticulously planned-out day. If something threatens to change the trajectory of my day, I am often met with increased anxiety, as I have to suddenly think on my toes. Survival mode kicks in—and I panic, frozen in place and unable to move forward.

In the past, I have allowed this to be an excuse to wallow in self-pity as I complained about the less-than-ideal state of my life. I realized this was getting me nowhere and, at best, I remained stuck right where I was. If I allowed this to continue, however, my situation could worsen, setting me even farther back than it already had. Sometimes, we have to remind ourselves how much we've learned and the value those lessons have not only in our lives, but in those we teach.

It's time to let go of being complacent in your current state. I get it—you are comfortable there and the thought of changing anything right now just isn't an option for you. If I sit and wallow in self-pity for losing my job, I won't ever find anything else to replace the income I have lost. But—if I keep trying, even in the face of rejection letters—to build a business that can help others, I am building a future I can be proud of while also leading in my area of expertise.

What if you could make a change right now that improves not only your current situation, but your future as well? No matter how afraid you are in this time of uncertainty, moving forward towards the next thing shows bravery. Be brave, friend.

Moving Forward with Hope

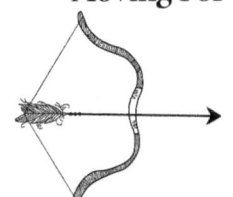

Change has the power to create resiliency in uncertainty.

Using your positive mindset when faced with a challenge will help you get through this trial and get back on top again.

How can you take everything you've learned and put it towards the transformation of your situation? Having the bravery to move forward with hope is an excellent place to start. The two other things you'll need are surrender and trust, which we are going to talk about in the next chapter.

Braver Choices

Actionable steps you can take to become braver with belief as you step into the role of servant leader. I have broken it down for you in a way that is easier to remember: B.R.A.V.E.R.

Brighten: An action taking call to service to refine our hearts as we discover the area in which to serve.

Serving Others: Go through your closet and purge items that no longer fit or you no longer wear. Donate them to a program in your area that supports a charity you can get behind.

Reflect: A prayer that covers the emotions felt within each chapter with a promise to let go of the things we need to, so we can keep moving forward.

> *Father, I am so sorry I didn't consider this change as your way of gently guiding me back on track. Help me let go of being frozen in place as stress and anxiety have taken over, and allow me to move forward again. Please forgive me for not trusting Your loving direction in my life. Amen.*

Act: An action taking exercise that forces us to get up and move forward.

Write a letter to your future self. Describe the changes you're currently experiencing and offer encouragement for what is coming. Write it as if you have already successfully navigated the change and reflect on how you have grown and adapted. Seal it in an envelope and pick a date in the future that you feel is allowing enough time to pass before you read this letter again. I recommend waiting six months to one year before you open the letter.

Verse: Memorization of a Bible verse that helps us remember the lesson within the chapter.

Write the following scripture and post it somewhere you'll see it every day; maybe a bathroom mirror, refrigerator, or your home office. Memorize it and refer to it when you feel afraid of the change before you.

> *"I the LORD do not change. So you, the descendants of Jacob, are not destroyed."*
>
> Malachi 3:6

Explore: An action taking exercise to help us explore new possibilities we may not have yet thought of.

Exercise: Make a list of past changes you have already overcome successfully. Include the steps you took to successfully get through.

Renew: A journal prompt for us to reflect with God in solitude.

Journal Prompt: Write your current fears about change. Next to each fear, rewrite it as a positive affirmation or strength. Example: I fear failure = I am learning and growing through each experience.

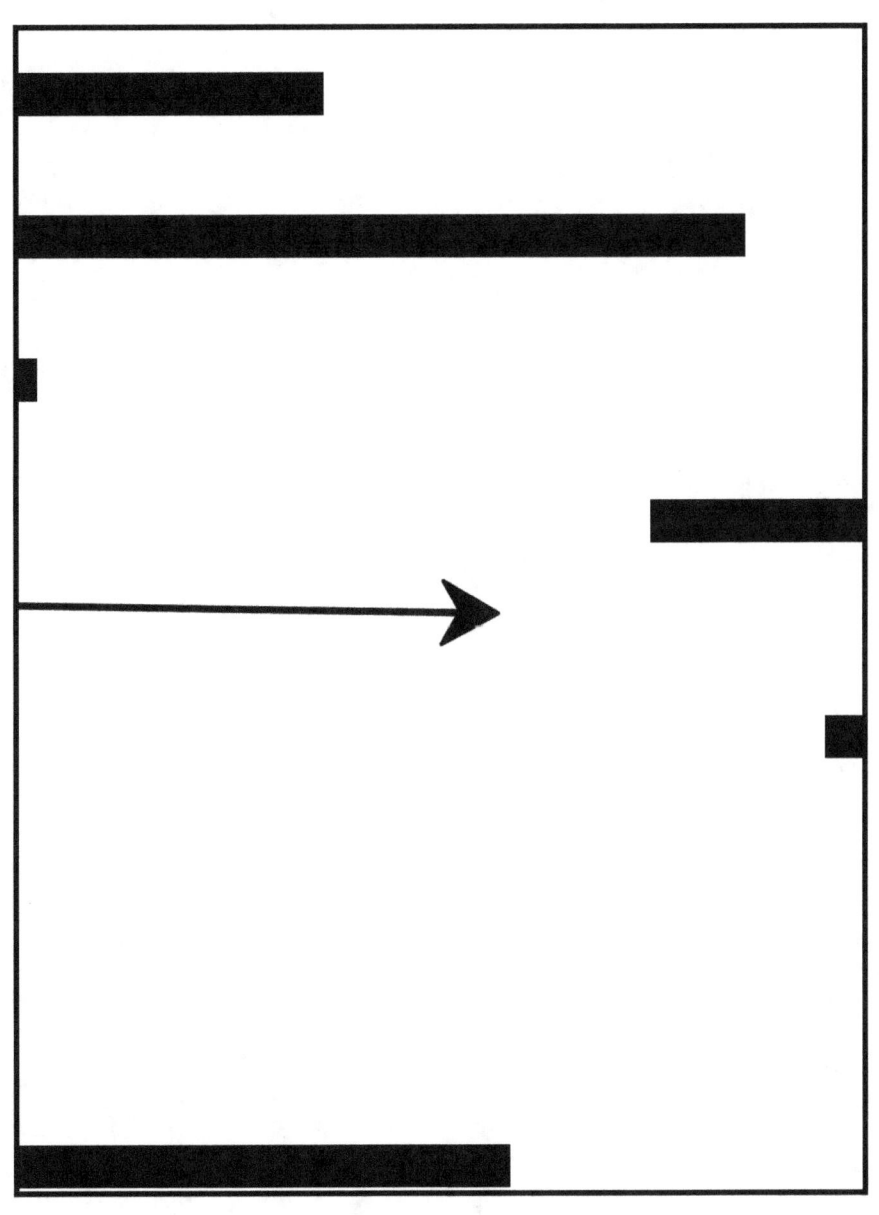

Chapter Nine

Surrender and Trust

Your bravery has brought you into uncharted territory. Where you once relied on others to guide you, you are now in a season of listening to God's direction. It's scary to trust your judgment, especially if you've made wrong choices before.

The thing I love about learning to trust my judgment is the time spent in prayer with God. When we pause before deciding, we allow space for God to enter into a conversation with us about the very thing we are considering. The act of pause keeps us from making an irrational decision.

How God guides you may look differently than how He guides me. His guidance isn't something I can explain other than it's a feeling I recognize as the Spirit moving within me. When I feel my decision is the right choice, I move quickly and trust that God is going to continue with me down the path I choose. Sometimes, I still get it wrong. But even when I do, I know God is with me during the consequences of my wrong decision as I correct the mistake.

When Things Don't Work Out

Earlier today, I ran my profit and loss summary for the current year-to-date totals to see where I was for the year. In comparison to last year, this year in particular has been a struggle. Frustrated, I took my glasses off and laid them on my desk so I could massage my forehead and eyes to soothe the tension headache brewing.

As I looked at the numbers in front of me, I wrestled with a decision I should have made years ago. When I first opened my business, I was concerned I wouldn't make enough compared to my corporate salary. The first few years were definitely a struggle.

I learned how incredibly difficult managing and bootstrapping a business was, while also analyzing data each month and comparing it to the previous year. Eventually, I got into the rhythm of making sure my performance was where I needed it to be. But in 2020, the world shut down, bringing a whole new list of problems.

With the rising costs in materials, I either had to take a loss or raise my prices to accommodate for the increases. I held out as long as I could, but in 2022, I had to increase my prices for the first time in five years. This change definitely affected the sales of my stationery goods.

I had no choice but to add a supplemental income by offering more design services as a freelancer to help ensure I was making enough to keep the business afloat. The problem I faced was the lack of time needed to keep the stationery brand going while I spent most of my working hours on client work. I also didn't have any extra time to work towards building a ministry focused on teaching that I felt called to build.

This new time management and financial struggle brought more stress and fear than the decision to go into business did. I began questioning whether this was the end of the stationery brand, or if there was something else I could do to help it survive. I can be extremely stubborn, and I refused to quit. When I face a challenge of this magnitude, I see it as an opportunity to learn a valuable lesson that can help me be a better business owner.

The problems in 2022 reminded me of similar discussions around profit margins from meetings at my previous job. Applying what I learned in those meetings, I developed and designed a CEO planner to help plan my business for the new year. To help grow my business, I explored additional revenue streams. This seemed to help as I saw my numbers in 2023 not only increase, but surpass what I had done in the past.

Until suddenly, sales were fewer, bookings slowed down, and I was right back to where I started. I had to make another change. I focused on publishing my first book, which was a risky decision, as it meant I had more money going out than coming in.

Between prioritizing my health and publishing my book, my time was stretched thin; I turned away new client work to maintain my current client roster. Now, as the end of the year rapidly approaches, I reflect on all the ways I fell short financially this year. It is painting a potentially grim picture for what may be coming next.

As I sit here today, during a fifteen-minute writing sprint with my writer's group, I must confess that even as the cheerful holiday music plays in the background, I am anything but cheerful. This chapter is a bit too real, too raw, and too current for my liking.

Writing about my current struggles is new to me, but I know it is important to share this moment with you, giving you the chance to see that even if we do everything right—there can still be trials that threaten to destroy our dreams. There can also be moments of triumph as we give in and allow our stubbornness to step aside long enough for God's goodness to take the lead.

I will be the first to admit I am very hard on myself. I dislike failing, and I have always been extremely resourceful. Which is why, as I looked over my numbers for the year, I knew it was time for me to step aside and possibly do something else. Even if that meant letting go of things that were important to me and make room for the things God was placing on my heart.

When I first started my business, my original business plan was God-centered. Everything I had envisioned. I wanted it to be hopeful, uplifting, inspirational, and Christ-like. Somewhere along the way, however, I shifted my business plan to accommodate the needs of others. I did not want to hurt their feelings or make them feel like they couldn't buy my products or use my services if they weren't Christians.

My decision to shift came from a place of wanting to be sensitive to the beliefs of others. In my life, people have pointed out that I can be overly enthusiastic when sharing my passions. I never realized that others might not receive my enthusiastic sharing of my beliefs well. When I am passionate about something, I enjoy discussing it—and sharing this side of me with others used to be something I did without pause. Now, I am a bit more apprehensive of my approach as I shrink my spirit to tiptoe around theirs.

As a result, I have had a tough time expressing who I am authentically, which included sharing scripture and stories from the Bible. I shied away from everything I had known as I wandered farther and farther away from God. It wasn't the fault of anyone this happened. It was a decision I had made slowly over time, without realizing it.

Recently, I admitted to a friend I felt like I was being disobedient by not sharing what was on my heart. She lovingly reminded me God gave us free will and maybe it wasn't time then, but it is now. I had to consider this thought for a moment as I looked at my current predicament with my business. I can't help but wonder if things could be different now, more successful even.

Had I not shifted my business plan in the beginning, would I have learned the same valuable lessons? Not wanting to pick up regret over the choices that brought me to where I am now, I have to look forward to where I'm headed. The only thing I can do now is give in and give up.

I'm not referring to "give in and give up" in the way you likely thought I meant. If I give in to the pressure and give up on my business, I may as well quit—and I refuse to quit. Let me share with you what I mean by choosing to give in and give up.

I choose to surrender my heart fully to God; I need to give in to Him as I invite Him to sit with me on this. A constant battle wages within me and against my desire to please those around me. Each time I'm knocked down, I immediately rise to meet the next challenge. Wouldn't it be better if I took a moment in-between to seek God's help? Perhaps if I did, I might escape these battles, as He'd bear the burden.

To trust God's direction, I need to give up the white-knuckled control I have over my business and trust He is going to direct me where He wants me to go. I must face the challenges this new direction presents. Although there are no guarantees, I know the outcome will be God's will for me. I can't argue with Him about this, because it will change nothing. The best thing I can do is trust He has my best interest at heart.

The moment I fully surrendered and put my trust in God, a shift took place within me. I now have a strong desire to make sure I am seeking God first in every decision I make. My prayer life used to consist of bedtime prayers, and falling asleep somewhere in the middle. Now, I have made daily conversations with God a priority. If I am unsure, I ask and sit quietly to wait and listen.

Surrendering Control

I prefer to be in control of everything to control the outcome. Lately, God has been teaching me how to trust Him and surrender my way to follow His. I used to view surrendering as weakness from giving in and giving up. In my stubbornness, I would dig my heels in and stand defiantly with my hands on my hips, declaring refusal to do the very thing I felt was the right thing to do. And falling flat on my face time and time again.

Eventually, when exhaustion sets in, you acknowledge that maybe your way isn't the right way after all, and fighting it isn't the answer. That time has come for me right now. The question is, what are my options for what is coming next? Earlier today, I pulled out my CEO planner for 2025 and worked through the guided prompts to set my brand planning for the new year. I took a long look at my website as I thoughtfully answered each question—and quickly realized a shift was taking place in the way I wanted to run my business in the new year.

I felt the gentle and loving nudge that came as a reminder of my initial business plan. Instead of arguing with God about the many reasons I felt I wasn't good enough to carry out His mission for me, I simply said, *"Okay, Lord, what will You have me do?"*

I sat in silence for a very long time. Perhaps I hoped I would hear an audible answer to the perplexing question I had just asked God, or maybe have some sort of epiphany that shined a light on the subject. Unfortunately, neither came, and my page remains blank until I know where to go from here. I may not know which direction I'm headed, but I know that a change is crucial now.

Recently, it seems I have been avoiding writing in my planner because part of me is fearing change and questioning if I am making the right decisions. I have tested the waters on what I believe I should transition my business to by creating an all new website interface. Not wanting to rush this process, I am giving myself the time I know I need to fully let go of how things once were, and open my heart up to new possibilities ahead.

It's difficult to close a door on something you nurtured and grew for eight years in honor of a life lost. Lilian Grace began to take the back seat in my business to make way for me to step forward as I presented myself as my brand. The vulnerability that came with me now being front and center was overwhelming. Was I disappointing Lilian Grace? In a way, I've always viewed my stationery brand as my baby, and letting it go feels like I'm losing my child all over again. Finding a happy medium to still honor the legacy I've created while making this transition is a delicate balancing act.

I can feel within my heart a more simplified approach is crucial at this stage. I have been doing far too much, which is catching up to me negatively. Simplified, however, worries me with finances. Mike always reminds me you can have time or money, but rarely can you have both. In my stubbornness, I tell him I will one day be able to have both—but I have yet to meet that one day.

Let Go

Being flexible and adaptable in the face of adversity is critical in helping your business survive. I recognize that in the past, I could not bend or adapt as I stood with my heels dug in, not moving a single inch. Perhaps the difference is that with time, God has continually molded me and shaped me through the various life lessons I was learning. He has given me the opportunity to become more resilient and confident in my approach to how I handle my business today.

I have learned the valuable lesson of surrendering my control and trusting that God will lead me down the path I am supposed to be on—while accepting it's not the path I want to be on. Despite having taken a wrong turn, God lovingly walked behind me, keeping a watchful eye as I stumbled and fell along the way. He was ever-patient, waiting for me to allow Him to help. There were days I would run so far ahead of Him I was fairly certain He wouldn't be able to catch up, only to become frightened as I searched frantically for Him in the darkness.

I don't know what the future holds for my business. But I know next year, I'm stripping it all down and going back to the basics. Simplifying not only my offerings, but expanding on them to be of service to others—that has always been one of my core values. As I take on a leadership role, I'll teach others the skills and knowledge I have gained over the years.

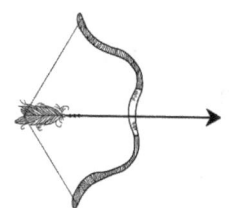 **I trust because of this alignment with God's purpose and will for my life, the seeds I have been planting will grow, allowing me to harvest them when the time is right.**

When I think about the original calling God placed on my heart at the age of nineteen, after attending a women's retreat—I get excited about the possibilities of dreaming big. In the past, I said I never had the time needed to put these ideas into practice. Now, I've realized I've kept myself so busy doing things I wanted to, I was ignoring the things God was asking me to work on.

Perhaps now is the time to let go of the things I am holding too tightly onto. There are other ways I can incorporate the memory of Lilian Grace into the future of my business to become more in alignment with God's idea for it. In a way, this further iterates the growth with each passing year. Just as kids don't stay young forever, neither do businesses as they continue to age with time. This thought no longer makes change feel terrifying, it is exciting and something that should be celebrated.

A clean slate feels like a new beginning, and this gives me a chance to adjust my strategy and grow my business to its full potential. When you adjust your thinking, you give yourself the chance to become excited about what you are building with God. Though I still ask for peer advice from time to time, every decision I make for my business is mine alone to make with God's guidance.

When a big change comes your way, don't be afraid. Surrender and trust God is going to see you through whatever you face. Be brave as you step to the side and allow God to lead you where you need to be. Ask yourself this important question—am I doing this for others or am I doing this for God?

The Unseen Truth

I stood in the darkness after losing God on the path I forged for myself. I realized I messed up. I also learned valuable lessons despite my mistakes—making my time worthwhile. Perhaps it's not that I messed up completely, but took a detour on my way to discovering something new.

What path are you currently traveling—the one you picked, or the one God asked you to take? I know it is sometimes difficult to discern who is guiding us when we listen to multiple voices about what we should or shouldn't do. Often, we ask others what they think we should do instead of asking God what He wants us to do. I know I am guilty of this, primarily because I am an extremely social person who values input from others. I have to remind myself, however, to spend time in solitude first and invite God to join me in these decisions.

If you haven't yet been able to fully surrender and trust God to lead you in the correct direction, have hope.

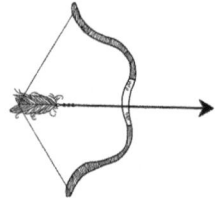

Surrendering isn't a sign of weakness, but an admirable strength that can only exist within someone who stands bravely in their faith.

What are you holding onto tightly that you need to let go of?

Braver with Belief

> *"But blessed is the one who trusts in the LORD, whose confidence is in him. They will be like a tree planted by the water that sends out its roots by the stream. It does not fear when heat comes; its leaves are always green. It has no worries in a year of drought and never fails to bear fruit."*
>
> Jeremiah 17:7-8

In order to become braver with belief, we have no other choice but to put all of our trust in God. Picture yourself as the tree in this verse, your roots going down by the stream to gather nutrients to help you grow stronger. You do not fear when trials come, for you have all that you need with you as you confidently face everything that comes your way.

If you struggle with being too stubborn or anxious to release control to the unknown, spend some extra time in solitude with God where you choose to be honest with Him about how you feel. Let Him know why you struggle with trusting that He has your best interest in mind. Perhaps you feel He's let you down in the past, which only contributes to your blind run as you continue to sprint down dark path after dark path, trying to run away from God.

No matter how fast and far you run, my friend, God will always be right behind you. You cannot outrun Him. May I recommend instead of running away from Him, you turn around and run to Him. God never promised us this life would be easy, but He did promise He will always be there for us when we call upon Him.

The Strength in Letting Go

Giving up control over my business isn't high on my priority list. Surrendering control and inviting God's guidance as I change direction evokes mixed emotions within me. The logical part of me thinks I'm crazy for blindly trusting God to manage crucial aspects of my business. However, a softer and faith-filled side of me feels hopeful, knowing that whatever happens next brings me closer to my purpose.

Though I may not see God physically sit next to me as I plan out my next year in business, I can absolutely feel Him at work in all I am doing. Just as I also know how it feels to not have Him sitting next to me as I carry out my business in a way that continually flops. I have had some really prosperous seasons, and looking back, I can identify the reason for those seasons was because He was next to me. I can also clearly see the years I struggled were the ones I stubbornly ignored His help as I tried to do it all on my own.

It's time to let go of the reins and allow God to join you. Perhaps you didn't even realize you stubbornly dug your heels in as you tried to do everything all on your own. Survival mode can kick in as we push through each day quickly to get us closer to where we want to be. Before we realize it, so much time has passed us as we do this daily—on repeat—until exhaustion catches up with us. You don't have to do that anymore, and neither do I.

When you face the unknown, do you trust and surrender, or hold on tightly as you control the situation? When you allow God to join in the space next to you, you are showing Him how much you trust Him as you surrender control to allow Him to direct you. I know this can be terrifying—but it can also be extremely rewarding.

Moving Forward with Hope

If what you have been doing all along isn't working any longer, perhaps it's time to surrender and trust God.

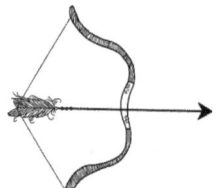

How would it feel to welcome in a sense of peace where once was stress?

By surrendering and trusting, you can reduce the overwhelm you are causing in your life as you live in a way that prioritizes leaning into God's guidance instead of running blindly. I don't know about you, but just the thought of that makes me feel so grateful for all God does for me. In the next chapter, we are going to talk more about what a spirit of gratitude can do for us as we become braver with belief.

Braver Choices

Actionable steps you can take to become braver with belief as you step into the role of servant leader. I have broken it down for you in a way that is easier to remember: B.R.A.V.E.R.

Brighten: An action taking call to service to refine our hearts as we discover the area in which to serve.

Serving Others: Offer to help someone without expectation of receiving anything in return. Chances are you know someone who could use an extra set of hands around the house to help clean up, paint, feed animals, take care of children, or something else.

Reflect: A prayer that covers the emotions felt within each chapter with a promise to let go of the things we need to, so we can keep moving forward.

> *Father, I am so sorry I kept running away from you, stubbornly trying to do everything on my own. Help me let go of the need to control my destination and trust your loving guidance. Please forgive me for not asking for your help sooner. Amen.*

Act: An action taking exercise that forces us to get up and move forward.

Draw a trust tree. Draw a tree with strong roots, branches, and leaves. Label the roots with things you are trusting God with. Write Bible verses on the leaves that reinforce trust.

Verse: Memorization of a Bible verse that helps us remember the lesson within the chapter.

Write the following scripture and post it somewhere you'll see it every day; maybe a bathroom mirror, refrigerator, or your home office. Memorize it and refer to it when you need a reminder to surrender and trust.

> *"Commit to the LORD whatever you do, and he will establish your plans."*
>
> Proverbs 16:3

Explore: An action taking exercise to help us explore new possibilities we may not have yet thought of.

Exercise: On a piece of paper, write things you are holding onto or controlling in your life. Once you've written them down, either tear it up or burn the paper.

Renew: A journal prompt for us to reflect with God in solitude.

Journal Prompt: Write about an area in your life where you're struggling with trust and surrender. Why is it so hard to let go?

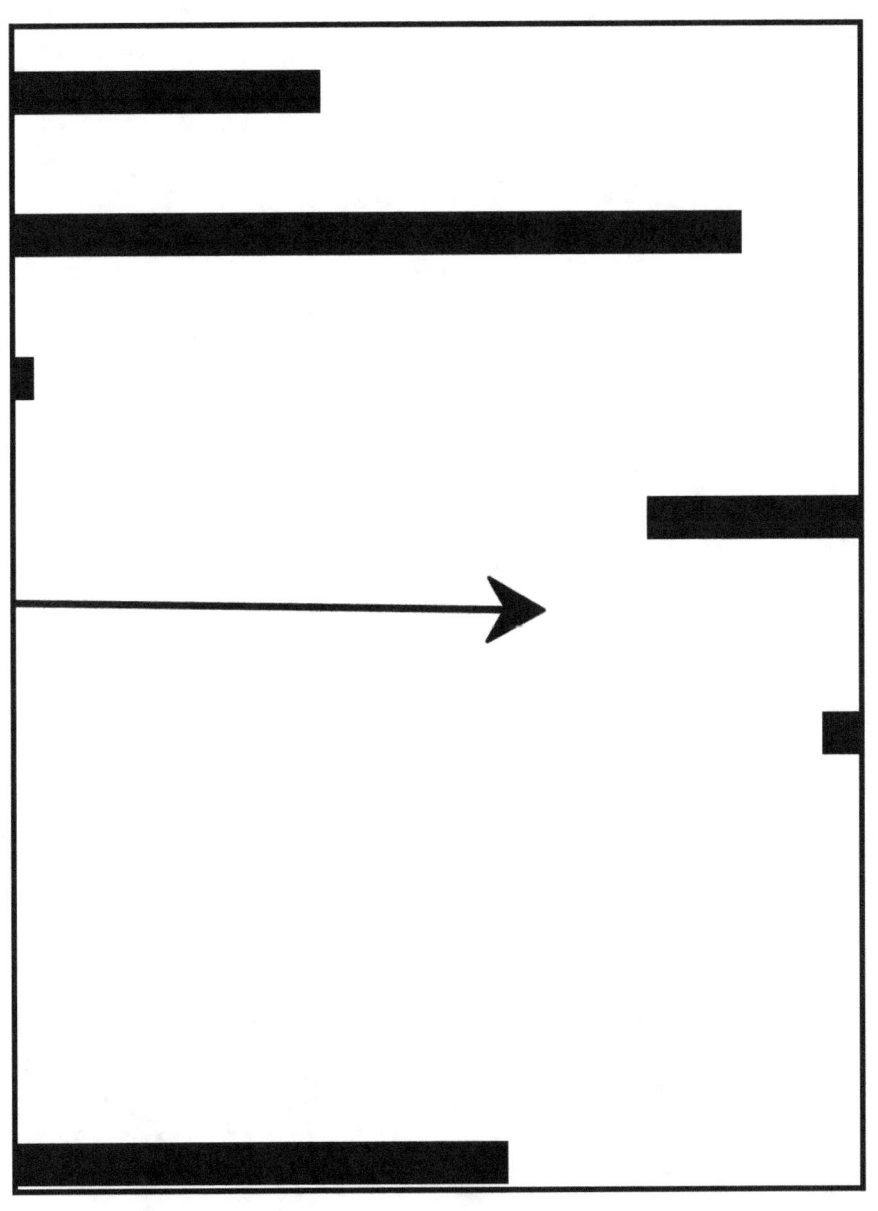

chapter Ten

A Spirit of Gratitude

For a long time, I struggled with trusting my own judgment. I know firsthand how hard it is to move forward confidently when I've made wrong choices. Let me remind you: we aren't perfect, nor are we expected to be. We will fail many times over. But do you want in on a little secret? Failure teaches us valuable lessons we can apply to our lives as we continue to grow.

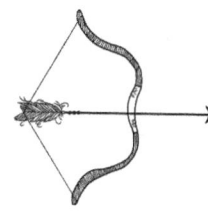

By fostering a spirit of gratitude—even when we fail, we recondition ourselves to think vastly differently than we have in the past.

Opening our hearts up to consistent moments filled with gratefulness, we reduce our stress and invite happiness to enter.

I don't know about you, but I could use a little more happiness in my life every day. Making the conscious effort to practice daily gratitude has helped me tremendously. When others do something for me—whether it is a word of encouragement, an acknowledgment, or a thoughtful gift—I have grown to enjoy expressing my gratitude immediately. Because I tend to be awkward and introverted in social settings, this has been a great challenge for me.

Grateful for Friendships

If you remember from earlier chapters, I have gotten used to sitting alone at home, wrapped up in a warm sherpa blanket, reading another cozy book. The older I get, the more I would rather be here than literally anywhere else. What I have grown to realize, however, is that while this may seem like a good idea, the lack of communication with others outside of my home eventually catches up to me. Loneliness creeps in and I begin to crave connection with others.

Before my life took twists and turns down some really dark and frightening paths, I was extremely social and delighted in spending time with family and friends. I hosted regular gatherings where we would stuff ourselves full of pizza and desserts while playing games and laughing all night long. We made memories I will cherish for the rest of my life. Even as I think about those memories now, I remember how much I have to be grateful for.

During our time as foster parents, we didn't get to do anything that wasn't directly tied to the children. I remember feeling alone in the new challenges and struggles we faced not only as foster parents, but as new parents of older children. We completely skipped the infant and toddler years. While I was grateful the children could tell me what they needed, I struggled with understanding fully whether I was a good mother as I passed out hand decorated goodie bags at the end of practice, chased them around the yard while dodging foam darts, or cleaned up the remnants of frozen grapes with Jello powder after snack time.

Even though there were challenges with fostering, there was much beauty that filled my life with joy. I met an incredible woman because of our children. We became friends almost instantly, and I always looked for her during every sporting practice. Meeting someone who was experienced with the demands of motherhood helped me ease into it more confidently. She was the first friend I made in the town we live in, and even though the children have long been gone, our friendship remains strong today. I am grateful for this wonderful friendship I formed during a time when I felt alone.

Grief crippled me after our children left and after my miscarriage. I had no desire to do things that once brought me joy. Instead, I poured myself into my career and took every opportunity I could to work overtime hours. However, my job loss made me confront what I'd been avoiding, only intensifying my grief.

I needed something, and was desperately searching for anything to keep my mind focused away the problems I was currently facing. I poured my heart into my new business. It breathed new life into me as I came up with ways to bring grace and hope to others who were hurting. When I couldn't process the pain I was experiencing, I wrote a card to encourage someone else who may also have felt a similar pain. I learned to be grateful for the hardships I endured, as they were the inspiration behind my stationery line.

Before long, I had a collection of cards that were resonating with customers. With every sale I made, I listened to stories from the thoughtful women who sent my cards to their friends. It showed me I could make a difference in a way I never believed I could. This discovery made me feel proud of sticking with it, even through grief and pain, and thinking outside of the box to help others who were hurting.

I realized I could not only survive one of the hardest seasons of my life, but I could also uplift others—despite feeling like I was drowning. I am grateful for starting my business; it pushed me to step outside of my comfort zone as I attended events and set up my products at stores. My business has allowed me to spend more time with old friends and make new ones as well.

When the world shut down three years after I started my business, I got comfortable in my stance of protecting my loved ones by saying no to invitations. Despite having been wildly successful with my brand, I was teetering on the edge of exhaustion from all the long hours I worked to keep the business going. Facing a pandemic for the first time in my lifetime brought up a whole new list of things I wish I had done differently, or things I still wanted to do.

Truth is, I was desperate for some alone time to sort through my jumbled thoughts about who I was and what I wanted out of life. The shutdown gave me the opportunity to work on myself and my relationship with God—but I wasn't ready to rejoin the crowd when things opened back up. I simply needed more time in solitude as I sought clarity within my relationship with God. Therefore, I continued to decline invitations to events and never corrected assumptions that my absence was related to Covid. Because of past rejections for being too religious or not religious enough, I was unsure how others would respond to the truth of needing more time alone with God.

I know my friends were disappointed when I declined the invitations they extended to me for those few years I took to rediscover myself. If I'm being honest, I hated saying no to my friends because I knew I needed them to fully heal. But I refused to dump my problems on their shoulders. Solitude allowed me to spend a lot of time being open and honest with God about my feelings concerning every stressful situation. Not holding back, I knew He would understand where I was coming from. I gradually felt better because I was confronting all the muck as I dumped my problems on His shoulders.

By spending the time working through my past problems, I could focus more and be present in my daily interactions with others instead of lost in thought about things I shouldn't focus on. Through it all, my friends never wavered as they patiently awaited my full return. I am grateful for being given the respectful space I needed to grow. It made me a more resilient woman and a much better friend than I had the capacity of being previously.

This past year, I have done the hard work of rebuilding my community after spending so much time in solitude. In doing this, I had a friend suggest I get back into setting up at events to sell my book alongside my stationery brand. I'll admit, at first I was terrified to put myself back out there—but once I made it through the first event successfully, it became something I looked forward to.

On the day of each event, I always started in prayer for the connections I would make throughout the event. I prepared my heart on the drive to the venue by worshipping the entire way there. Once fully set up, I would walk around, observing other vendors and connecting with other authors and entrepreneurs.

My favorite part of putting myself back out there again was that I had a great friend who set up beside me. She was the one who encouraged me to do this again. And I know she encouraged me because she knows me enough to know what I needed—usually before I did. I am extremely grateful not only for her encouragement to try again, but also for her unwavering support and friendship over the years. I haven't always been the best friend she deserves, but I hope she knows how loved and appreciated she is.

Those events taught me the importance of connecting with others and sharing God's word. I connected with women reading my book, and listened as they shared their struggles, telling me how much of an impact my book, *Authentically Anchored*, had on them. These new friends were connecting with who I am authentically. I am grateful for strangers giving me a chance and taking time to get to know me.

The lessons I've learned from my new friends have been the driving force behind the making of this book. There are so many people praying for guidance on what their next step in life should be. What I'd like to impart to you now, is the courage to feel gratitude again.

As you weather the storms of life, it is easier to hide from the world as you sort through things. Putting yourself back out there can be uncomfortable, but there are so many amazing opportunities that arise when you do. I challenge you to look at things in a different light. It will create a mindset shift that changes dissatisfaction to a spirit of gratitude.

Be grateful for the friends who encourage you to try again. They may not simply be pushing you to do something you don't want to do. They are gently reminding you of the things you once loved and perhaps have stopped doing without putting much thought into it. Often, our friends don't know exactly what to do to help us get through the things we are struggling with. If it is someone you have fully welcomed into your life, they likely know you enough to view your situation from a different perspective.

If what you are doing is no longer working, perhaps give their recommendations a try. You may find it opens up your heart, and it might also strengthen the bond between you and your friend. If I have learned anything, it is that time is extremely precious. We cannot get back the time we've lost by shutting everyone out. What we can do is start living each new day by showing our gratitude for those we love.

Be grateful for opportunities to make new friends, meet new people, learn new things, and overflow your memory bank. If you aren't actively living life, it will pass you by so quickly. Once you step outside and begin to fully live again, you'll discover a whole new world awaits you.

Ways to Express Gratitude

I shared with you one of the easiest ways to express gratitude: by telling someone you are grateful for them or what they have done for you. This simple act of gratitude reiterates that the recipient feels seen and heard for what they have done. It goes much farther than a simple thank you, especially when you tell them why you are grateful for them.

Another way you can express gratitude is by journaling your experiences and describing why you are grateful for them. Looking back on this later will remind you of your many blessings. This method is great for keeping a log of things you may otherwise forget as you come back and revisit it in the future.

Writing a letter to God, sharing the many ways in which you are grateful for things He has done in your life, is a great way to connect to God in solitude. You can use writing to keep a record of blessings, then tuck them away in your Bible to rediscover later. When I am going through a hard time, I love flipping through my Bible and finding all the notes I have hidden in it throughout the years. Adding the date will remind you of that moment when you find it again.

Another fun and meaningful thing to do is at the end of each day, focus on three good things that happened that day and express gratitude for them. This exercise keeps you present and mindful each day. And by doing it each evening, you will go to sleep focused on happy thoughts.

This will also aid in working on your mindset and presence as we discussed in chapter seven.

Experiment and find what best works for you to maintain a consistent habit of expressing gratitude daily. The more you do it, the easier and more natural it becomes. It is also a good idea to note the shift in mindset you'll undoubtedly have once you do this. This shift is another example of something you can be grateful for. By having a spirit of gratitude, you'll become a leader with a natural positivity that draws others to you.

Gratitude is Powerful

Now that I am back into setting up at events and selling my products, I have enjoyed looking for events with good success rates as I ease back in. Imagine my surprise, however, when a few of these events weren't as successful as predicted. Defining my idea of a successful event involves selling enough product to get my booth fee, plus the cost of items sold back—at a minimum. When my expectation of breaking even isn't met, I face a decision. I can respond negatively, expressing my frustration because of the lack of money made, or I can respond gratefully, rejoicing in the new connections I made with those who did shop with me.

The old way of thinking comes from a place of lack, where I would focus on the negative aspects of my experience. If left unchecked, the negativity would grow and spread like a wildfire as it torched the joy I once held within. If I truly want to become braver with belief, I can only respond out of the abundance of my heart, where I am excited for the connections made—whether or not they had monetary value.

By responding with a grateful heart, I remained excited for the next event and discovering who I could meet and learn about. I made it a priority to seek at least one new vendor at each show to meet and get to know. Making new connections with like-minded individuals showed me there is room in my life for new friends. I have been wanting to expand my friendship circle a bit, and this was a great opportunity for me to do so. As a result, I ended my year with several new friends who I am excited to grow alongside. I am extremely grateful for all the events I attended. The amount of growth I had as a result is something I will take with me for a very long time.

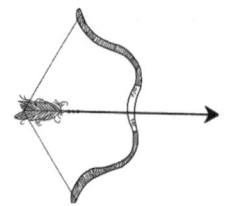

Gratitude has flipped the script on me, taking me from seeing what I don't have and showing me what God has already done.

In revealing His faithfulness, it solidifies to me that when troubles arise, God will be faithful again. The more I express my gratitude to God for the goodness in my life, the more I notice Him and all He is doing around me. Sometimes I feel I don't earn the blessings He's given me, but knowing He felt I did makes me more humble.

Take some time today to consider all the ways God has been faithful in your life. Express your gratitude to Him for blessing you, even if you feel you didn't deserve it.

The Unseen Truth

I had to stop dwelling on negative thoughts and feelings to shift my perspective to come from a place of gratitude. I often struggled with this concept because the trials in my life felt so complex and weighed me down. It was easier to seek the joy in each situation than it was to find something to be grateful for within it. I started my gratitude journey by recognizing the individuals who made me feel seen, heard, and understood by simply supporting me.

Can you identify who has been there for you during your hardest days? I quickly saw how my friends supported me in the direst of situations. This realization automatically shifted my thinking to how grateful I was for them. I had some friends who walked away when my life got difficult and messy. They felt it was easier to distance themselves from me than it was to help me find solid ground again. Those relationships are long gone—but in their wake, they gave me the opportunity to be more vulnerable with the friends who stayed.

If you haven't yet been able to identify a friend who has always remained faithful, perhaps shift your mindset a bit to stop focusing on those who left you and search for the faces of those who tried to be there for you, even if you didn't allow them to be.

Who is someone you are grateful for, and why?

Braver with Belief

"Give thanks in all circumstances; for this is God's will for you in Christ Jesus."
1 Thessalonians 5:18

In order to become braver with belief, having a spirit of gratitude changes our perspective in our everyday encounters. When I look back at a storm I've weathered, I am not always filled with gratitude for the trials I endured, but I am grateful for those who sat in the rain beside me. Going through the trials I have faced were valuable life lessons that severely altered the woman I was becoming. God brought others into my life at just the right time. Whether they became a good friend or were simply a complete stranger passing with a kind word, it helped me appreciate all I have.

If you are currently weathering a storm, it may be difficult to put this into practice with what is happening right now. I would encourage you to try practicing gratitude with something from your past that you have overcome and can now look at with a fresh perspective. Perhaps by discovering gratitude hidden in the past, it could be the start of a mindset shift needed to see something you can be grateful for in today's storm.

Once you identify the individuals who have shared their unwavering love and support with you, may I encourage you to show them how grateful you are for them? In addition, share with God the many ways you are grateful He brought them into your life. Remember your friends in prayer; you never know when they may need you during their hardships. May you never again take for granted the kindness they've shown to you as you live each day to its fullest again.

The Strength in Letting Go

Do you remember from the last chapter how I confessed I was stubborn? This trait of mine also makes me shortsighted. In my stubbornness, the way I think about the situations I find myself in becomes increasingly more negative as I cannot find a way out. The only way to combat a negative mindset is by reversing it to become a more positive one, as we learned in chapter seven. To help keep us in this positive mindset for longer periods of time, we can do so by fostering a spirit of gratitude.

Trials make it harder for us to be grateful for things in our life when our world feels like it's crumbling all around us. This added challenge pushes us outside of our comfort zone as we search for anything that gives us a glimmer of hope. It takes practice and repetition to find gratitude during a trial, so don't give up if you struggle at first.

It's time to let go of the tunnel vision you've grown accustomed to every time you face a difficult situation. Remove the blinders so you can look at your world around you. Will you still see a dumpster fire before you? Probably. But you'll also likely see the kindness and love that is standing next to it with an extinguisher. Once you've had help to put the fire out, you'll be able to sit down with your friend and talk about how much fun you just had together battling the flames.

When was the last time you gave thanks for your trials? We don't yet know that the trials we are facing are also helping establish resiliency and confidence within us. By viewing these trials with a spirit of gratitude, we take the negative and shift it to a positive lesson that we can not only learn and grow from—we can use those lessons to help others through theirs. Give thanks to God for sending others to you to help you when you need it most. Who knows, this new spirit of gratitude within you may also open the door for you to serve a friend during their time of need, too.

Moving Forward with Hope

Expressing gratitude for those who have supported you strengthens your bond with them as they feel seen, heard, and appreciated for the role they had in helping you. When was the last time you reciprocated that help to your friends during their time of need? This delicate balance of give and take among friends promotes unity as we look forward to a more hopeful future. I can't wait to talk more about this in the next chapter.

Braver choices

Actionable steps you can take to become braver with belief as you step into the role of servant leader. I have broken it down for you in a way that is easier to remember: B.R.A.V.E.R.

Brighten: An action taking call to service to refine our hearts as we discover the area in which to serve.

Serving Others: Consider someone who recently did something for you, either by encouragement or act of service. Express your gratitude to them by sending them a card in the mail.

Reflect: A prayer that covers the emotions felt within each chapter with a promise to let go of the things we need to, so we can keep moving forward.

> *Father, I am so sorry that I blindly focused on my trials and how they were affecting me instead of seeing all the goodness that surrounded me despite it all. Help me let go of the negative outlook I place on the trials I face. Please forgive me for not appreciating the friends you brought to me, and acknowledging all they have done for me throughout the years. Amen.*

Act: An action taking exercise that forces us to get up and move forward.

Make a list of friends you are grateful for and why you are grateful for them. Be specific in writing what they did. Keep your list as a reminder of how amazing your friends are. Put it somewhere where you will cross paths with it again and again.

Verse: Memorization of a Bible verse that helps us remember the lesson within the chapter.

Write the following scripture and post it somewhere you'll see it every day; maybe a bathroom mirror, refrigerator, or your home office. Memorize it and refer to it when you struggle to find gratitude on hard days.

> *"I thank my God every time I remember you. In all my prayers for all of you, I always pray with joy because of your partnership in the gospel from the first day until now."*
> Philippians 1:3-5

Explore: An action taking exercise to help us explore new possibilities we may not have yet thought of.

Exercise: Go for a walk outside. Pick up a rock as soon as you get started and hold that rock the whole time you walk. As you hold it, think about one specific blessing you are grateful for. Each time you move a finger across it or feel its weight, remember this blessing. When you get back home, write the blessing either on the stone or on a piece of paper and keep it with the rock in a place where you will regularly see it. Every day thereafter, when you see it, give thanks for something new.

Renew: A journal prompt for us to reflect with God in solitude.

Journal Prompt: Write three things you are grateful for. Go into as much detail as possible to capture the reason you are grateful.

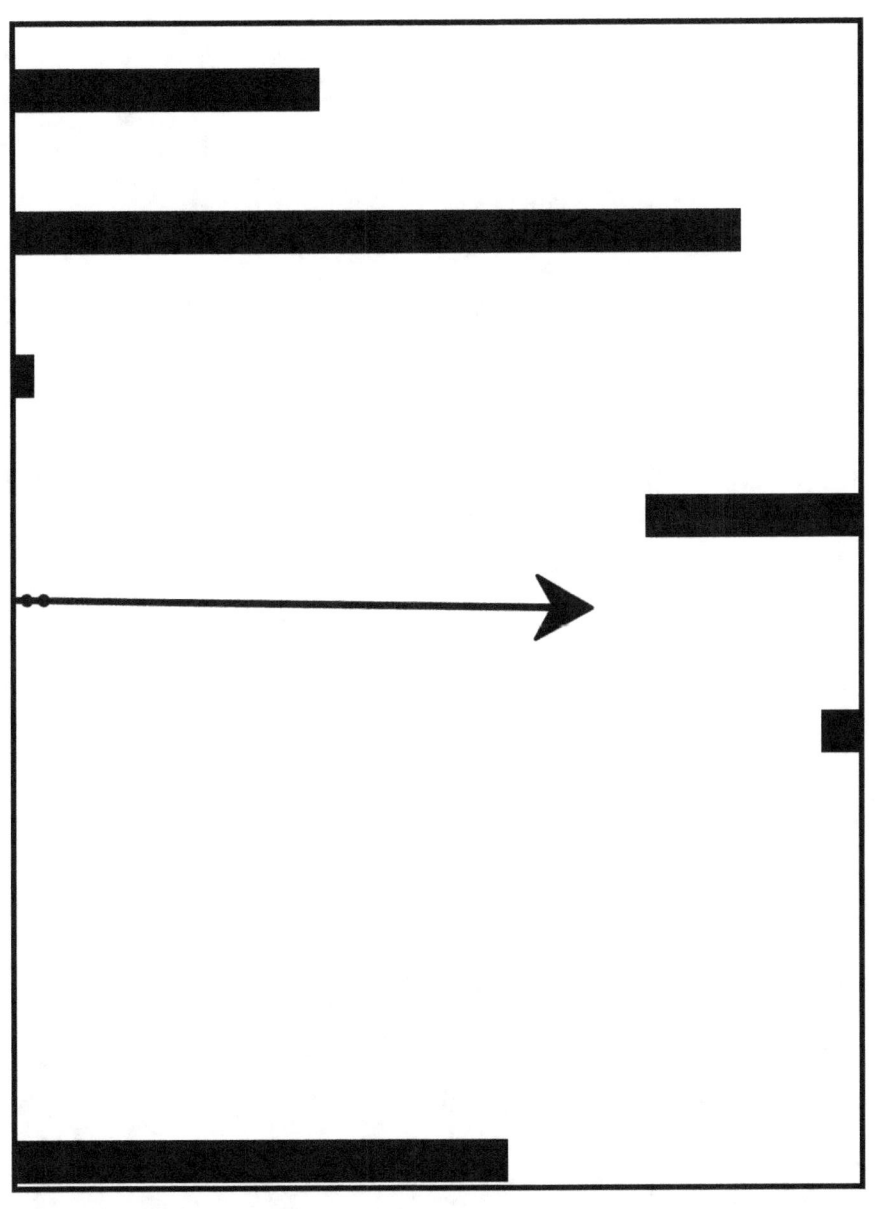

Chapter Eleven

Hopeful Future

ᴛᴏ ꜱᴇᴇ more good in the world today, change is essential. And it begins within you.

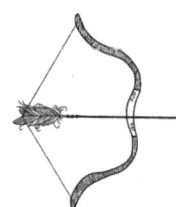

If you are unwilling to change into the woman God is calling you to be, you cannot be the servant leader others need.

By applying everything you've learned so far, you should feel a significant shift as God draws nearer to you. The old way of doing things like relying on the opinions of others, trying to take control of your situation, and holding onto grudges is no more. The new refined way of life you are living is one with purpose, intent, and a closer walk with God.

The change occurring within you is promising. It gives room for hope to enter as you consider the possibilities your future may hold. Contemplate for a moment the people God is preparing to be served by you. It's time to prepare your heart to serve them for Him.

October 2024 | The Concert

The buzz in the air felt stronger than any form of electricity I have ever felt in one area at one time. We arrived early, and when we first walked in to locate our seats, the arena was scarce. This was the first concert I had attended in many, many years—but was one that was on my bucket list for a very long time. The concert was a gift from a dear friend for my birthday and Christmas. I still cannot believe she pulled off such a thoughtful surprise and how she went above and beyond to make the evening special.

Normally, I would feel uneasy in crowded spaces as my anxiety would creep in and make me survey the nearest exits to escape and catch my breath when needed. However, there was something different about this experience—and the concert hadn't even started. We chatted excitedly with the seat mates directly behind us and posed for photos in front of the empty stage. Of course, the seats my friend surprised me with were directly right to the stage. It lent a perfect view not only of the stage, but the center stage runner that led out into the middle of the arena.

The opening act came out and the whole arena filled with familiar melodies as people started pouring in to find their seats. I took notice of the crowd as laughter permeated the space. Everyone seemed to be just as excited as I was to be there, yet I couldn't help but still feel a tad self-conscious about my size as we took our seats in the crowded row.

Typically, I would allow these negative thoughts about myself to be the driving force behind whether I would enjoy myself. However, this was a very special moment in time. One to be cherished for the rest of my life. I refused to allow my negative thinking to ruin the moment. I looked around to see the faces of everyone near where I was sitting. Instantly, I felt a warm sense of welcoming as I received smiles from others similar in size to me, sitting just a few feet from me.

The second act took the stage—and while it was a good performance, I was growing more excited about the featured artist yet to come. When the announcer asked us to all turn on our cell phone flashlights and hold up our phones, I held my breath. I took in all the lights shining around me—and it was absolutely stunning.

With a quick intermission to reset the stage, my friend and I posed for more photos with the new stage setup and chatted with our neighbors about the excitement we all shared about the featured guest.

Others who've attended these concerts shared with me I was in for a real treat, which only added to my growing excitement and curiosity.

I was busy watching people on the floor posing for photographs with each other when I noticed someone was recording something up high in the rafters. Just as I looked up, the concert began as the star of the show jumped off of the sign in the rafters while tied to a bungee cord. The entire crowd erupted in cheers. Now, I don't know about you, but I get out of breath when dancing. I cannot carry a melody on-key while dancing back and forth, let alone bouncing up and down at the speed she was moving. It was absolutely incredible to watch the artistry in her performance.

I thoroughly enjoyed myself throughout the whole concert as I joined in and sang along with the songs I knew—which were pretty much all of them. At one point in the concert, I stood in awe and watched as she stood really close to where we were standing and chatted with her audience as if we were all her best friends. Her positivity and joy were absolutely infectious, permeating the walls in the vast space and wrapping around us like sunshine on a warm summer day.

Tears filled my eyes as I watched her perform aerial acrobatics high above, in the most beautifully artistic way I've ever seen in my entire life. Her dance crew was the most talented group I have ever seen on one stage; they moved seamlessly as if they were one complete unit, fully relying on each other. I found myself overcome with emotion. Suddenly, it dawned on me that the feeling I was experiencing directly resulted from seeing teamwork and acceptance in a beautiful real-life demonstration right before my eyes.

Although people know this artist for her controversial demeanor and outspokenness, they should also celebrate the love she shares with those around her. She reminded me it's okay to stand firm in what you believe while still also loving others—despite the differences you may have. Perhaps she was the exact person I needed to help open my eyes and see an example of what it is like to lead in love.

I scanned the audience to see if I could determine what they were also feeling in this moment—and I was met with love, admiration, and pure joy. It is difficult for me to put into words exactly what this moment meant to me. Though time didn't stand still, it felt as if I was in a place where time ceased to exist. I had forgotten what it felt like to live life carefree and fully present in the moment, without fear of judgment or criticism. As I smiled at the stranger next to me, I couldn't help but feel a kindred spirit in her as she returned my smile.

This indescribable feeling was so evident to me, I could only recognize it as a prompting from the Holy Spirit. This inner prompting made me sit and think about the ministry I wanted to lead. To best serve those who come to me, I need to ensure my heart is open to accepting them as they are, at their most authentic selves. My head needed to be freed from casting judgment towards others for choices they've made in their lives. I realized the best way to serve others is to do so as Jesus would have done.

We All Want Acceptance

At one point in my life, I was interested in studying other religions to fully understand what made them different from Christianity. This was also a way for me to determine my beliefs and how strongly I felt about them, while also understanding my friends and their beliefs. I used to think I had it all right, and they had it all wrong. Until one day, I realized, perhaps I was wrong to believe that way—and though most religions are different, they have similar principles.

As I tried to understand these differences, I felt God opening my heart to acceptance. It doesn't matter what color my skin is or the extra weight I carry. Accepting another human being, different in appearance than I am, truly matters—because it's who God created them to be. Recognizing my friend's disbelief in Christianity, I also respected her personal beliefs while acknowledging our differences.

Attending this concert reminded me that connection with each other is something to celebrate as we all grow together toward a more hopeful future. I have never felt more welcomed anywhere on earth than I did in that arena. There is no church that I have stepped foot in, no home, no event, no place except that night that I felt truly at peace with everyone around me as we all sang, let loose and danced, and tilted our heads back to laugh together.

It was as if time itself stood still and as the confetti fell all around me. As she performed the final number, I tilted my head back and praised God for the biggest lesson on acceptance I have ever learned in my entire life. After the concert, a huge smile covered my face. I finally understood Jesus's meaning of "love one another."

Attending a secular artist's concert unexpectedly unveiled a whole new depth of God's love for me. In the past, I would have listened to others tell me that as a Christian, we shouldn't partake in such things. But I'm so glad that God created me to dare to be different, to experience new things that provide me with the chance to see so much clearer His goodness all around me. God will use every opportunity He can to bring us closer to Him, if we will only allow Him.

Love Like Jesus

Friend, this world has become so divided that we are missing out on relationships with incredible people that God brings into our lives. I don't know about you, but I wouldn't want anyone other than God judging me for my sins, so why are we so quick to judge?

I think back to what the scriptures share when talking about the relationships Jesus had with his followers. It makes me want to live my life more like He did; open, honest, and accepting of others. If I could do anything at all, it would be to show others how loved they are, hoping they feel the love of Jesus through me.

I know that this isn't how I have lived my life up to this point, but I also know that change begins with me. That change had already begun before the night of that concert, but grew increasingly intense after. I can't help but wonder how much more beautiful this world would be if we all loved each other like Jesus.

Let me remind you: learning about how others believe won't cause harm to who you are as long as you remain steadfast in truth and love through the Scriptures. Studying other cultures and religions has been absolutely fascinating to me, and this continuous learning fosters greater acceptance of others.

I remember times when others judged my weight and appearance, and I longed for their acceptance and loving kindness. That feeling fuels my interactions with others, keeping me open to the possibilities of beautiful friendships with others I meet. So many people are trying to find their seat at a table where they feel comfortable. I want to pull back a chair for them, welcoming them to my table.

While I stand firm in my stance that it isn't my job to point out the sin of others, it is my calling to help them through their struggles as they seek guidance. The difference between addressing their sin without permission and walking alongside them when asked, is one comes from a spirit of condemnation, while the other comes from a spirit of compassion. I openly share scripture as I feel led to do so. I ask if I can pray for them or with them, and I will always remind them that God loves them as they are.

Don't be afraid to share what is in your heart, even if your beliefs differ. Authentically open up and be transparent in a way that truly reflects God's love in and through you to those who are accepting it. Some may not be comfortable hearing these things, and that's okay too.

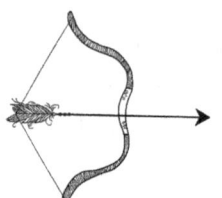

You can be respectful of others' beliefs while still honoring yours.

People are hurting, confused, and angry. Those three traits are not anything that comes from God. The king of confusion is winning because we allow him to defeat us. The best way to fight back is by leading with love and kindness.

Preparing Your Heart

Every day since that concert, I have prayed for God to prepare my heart to love like Jesus. Although the world remains divided, my conviction to be united persists. I consider what heaven will be like when I arrive, and that fuels my desire to help others see they can be a bridge, too.

God is calling His army to prepare. The number of conversations I have had recently on this very subject is too great to count. Many women within my network are feeling called right now to serve in some capacity. Some do not know how or what they are being called to do, but have undeniably felt the push to lead.

Women reach out to me for help with putting together their branding and strategy to make progress towards their ministry. Each time I send them homework, I tell them all the same thing—invite God to join you before you do this. Asking God to prepare your heart as you obediently step into a season of servant leadership is exactly what you should do right now.

Answering Your Calling

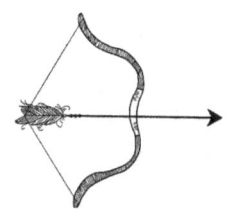 **Knowing God is calling you to be a servant leader is less about an obvious revelation and more about a deep, persistent stirring within your spirit.**

A steadfast desire to lead by lifting others, love sacrificially, and serve with humility becomes present.

How do you know God is calling you to be a servant leader? The answer to that lies within your spirit. I cannot confirm or deny God has placed a calling on your heart. What I have found in my own calling is a deep desire to help others grow. Suddenly, I need to step aside as I *teach* others more than I *do* for others.

Rather than designing for others, I feel I am ready to teach others how to design for themselves. This example merely scratches the surface of what my calling is, but gives you an example of what to pay attention to within your heart.

I find as I pray, I often ask God to use me each day. I have surrendered in a way that lends God the chance to direct me where He needs me. As a result, people, opportunities, and scripture have shown up at just the right time. With each new discovery, it is further confirmation that I am on the right path; the one God has set before me.

As I say yes to my calling, I feel a conviction to lead by example, not just words. Looking back, I can see where I struggled to do things that I have asked you to do throughout this book, such as when I was relying on asking the opinions of my friends instead of deciding on my own, letting go of the regret and shame I've carried, and leading in love when connecting with those whose beliefs differ from my own

Your calling may cause a sense of hesitation within you. If you are unsure of what to do, I encourage you to draw nearer to God, and ask Him to use you. Remain vigilant to what comes next. The enemy will do everything he can to stop you from fulfilling your calling. Look for opportunities that may arise with new connections and opportunities as God points you in the right direction.

Choose to say yes to your call to become a servant leader, as it fills all our futures with hope. When you bravely step forward to share your gifts with others, you can help change their lives for the better. Whether you are called to start a business, write a book, start a ministry, or simply offer a helping hand, your call has merit. God has chosen you. Thank you for your obedience to follow God's direction.

The Unseen Truth

With an open heart and mind, I allowed myself to experience something new that was completely outside of my comfort zone. In attending the concert, I received one of my life's biggest lessons yet on acceptance. There wasn't a single moment at the concert that I feared I was in danger from anyone at the concert, despite us all being extremely different in appearance, ethnicity, and beliefs. Quite the opposite happened. And for the first time in my life, I felt seen and welcomed.

When you meet someone who believes differently than you, have you fully taken the time to understand them and why they believe the way they do? Accepting others goes deeper than just saying you accept them as they are. Getting to know who they are, being invested in learning what you can about their beliefs or culture, and supporting their efforts are all part of acceptance. If you simply state you accept them but turn and walk away, you aren't fully accepting them as you close off your heart.

If you wish to see a change in this world in how we treat one another, let me remind you that change begins with you. You can choose to lead by example as you open your home to others and welcome them to their seat at your table. Who knows—you may just save a life that was on the verge of extinction because of their personal struggles. That, my friend, would be a beautiful thing, indeed.

What does 'loving one another as God has loved you' mean to you?

Braver with Belief

"My command is this: Love each other as I have loved you. Greater love has no one than this: to lay down one's life for one's friends."
John 15:12-13

In order to become braver with belief, we must set aside our differences as we lead in love and acceptance of others. To lay down your life for your friends could mean to stop worrying about what others may say or think about you being friends with someone who is different as you welcome them into your home and circle. I don't know about you, but when people come over to my house, we don't sit around discussing all the millions of ways we differ from each other. Instead, we focus on the moment as we laugh and have fun together, doing things we all enjoy.

If you know someone who usually gets left out of the party because they are different, get to know them more and see if there is some common ground you share that creates a new friendship. You may be the only person to have ever taken a chance on them, and that decision to do so will have a lasting impact for years to come. We all want to be loved and accepted by others.

Have you ever felt rejected by others because you are different? Allow that feeling to propel you as you change how you lead in love. Even if you try and the friendship goes nowhere, at least you'll have tried to show God's love to someone who needed it.

The Strength in Letting Go

There is so much division in the world that is splitting the masses. But one common thread: we are all sinners, born imperfect, and blessed with free will. Loving one another like Jesus is best represented in the story where He washes His disciples' feet in John 13. Imagine Jesus looking Judas in his eyes as He washed his feet, knowing that soon, Judas would betray Him. Despite this, He chose this moment to show Judas how much He accepts and acknowledges him in this one act of love, while simultaneously teaching us all a new command: *"A new command I give you: Love one another. As I have loved you, so you must love one another."* John 13:34

It is because of this command I choose to lead in love and acceptance of all individuals. I am not the judge. All I can do is show the love of Jesus through my actions to those who need it and are open to receiving it. Although I'm imperfect at this and often miss the mark despite my best efforts, I never stop trying. When people need space, I give it to them and let them choose if they still want my company, despite our differences. I want everyone to feel comfortable authentically being themselves around me, and not at all like they have to be someone they aren't.

It's time to let go of contributing to the division that is exploding in the world today. You have the freedom and power to come to your own conclusion about how things really are versus how they seem to be. Don't be so quick to write someone off by judging them harshly, without giving them a chance to prove to you who they are. Be an example of God's love in and through you to all you meet. Because we have the love of the Lord in us, we lead differently.

Who have you encountered and dismissed quickly—and now wish you could get to know? If you are in a place where you can be open to learning more about them and their beliefs, I encourage you to start there. As you hear them out, do not debate their beliefs or question them in a demeaning way. It's okay to ask questions that lead to more teachable dialogue to understand one another. This doesn't mean that you plan to change your stance or your beliefs, but it's a way for you to understand where they are coming from so you can learn how to best love them.

Moving Forward with Hope

Being the change this world needs means to lead in love. Say yes to the calling God is placing on your heart to be a servant leader. Focus on setting the example by letting others see God work in and through you without condemning them or their actions. By allowing yourself to love like Jesus, you become braver with belief more than ever, as you become more reliant on God and less reliant on others, which is the topic of our next chapter.

Braver Choices

Actionable steps you can take to become braver with belief as you step into the role of servant leader. I have broken it down for you in a way that is easier to remember: B.R.A.V.E.R.

Brighten: An action taking call to service to refine our hearts as we discover the area in which to serve.

Serving Others: Connect with someone whose beliefs differ from yours. Ask them questions, get to know why they believe the way they do. Do not impress your beliefs on them. Remember, you asked to hear their side. Do so with an open heart and quiet lips. You may not agree with how they believe, but you'll know more about why they believe the way they do. Being respectful of the differences you possess goes a really long way. By actively listening, you are showing them that you reserve a safe space to share their vulnerabilities with you. Remember that leading others to Christ is a long-term commitment and doesn't happen overnight.

Reflect: A prayer that covers the emotions felt within each chapter with a promise to let go of the things we need to, so we can keep moving forward.

> *Father, I am so sorry I was quick to judge others who differ from me. Help me let go of the need to be right in my stance and open my heart up to learn about the differences in others. Please forgive me for not being an example of your love in and through me. Amen.*

Act: An action taking exercise that forces us to get up and move forward.

Have a group discussion with friends of different backgrounds. Set boundaries ahead of time with all invited guests that this is to be an open and respectful discussion to simply learn from each other. Discuss how it's possible to disagree on opinions while still respecting and accepting core values that others have. This helps build mutual respect and understanding despite differing views.

Verse: Memorization of a Bible verse that helps us remember the lesson within the chapter.

Write the following scripture and post it somewhere you'll see it every day; a bathroom mirror, refrigerator, or your home office. Memorize it and refer to it when you struggle to love someone who frustrates you.

> *"Above all, love each other deeply, because love covers a multitude of sins."*
>
> 1 Peter 4:8

Explore: An action taking exercise to help us explore new possibilities we may not have yet thought of.

Exercise: After you've learned multiple new view points, choose one person who has different beliefs or opinions than you. For one week, try to see the world through their eyes. Journal your thoughts, feelings, and the challenges of seeing things from a new angle. In no way during this exercise should you do anything that doesn't align with your own faith walk and core values. This is simply an exercise to view things from their perspective to understand.

Renew: A journal prompt for us to reflect with God in solitude.

Journal Prompt: Write about a time when you met someone with beliefs or opinions that differed significantly from your own. How did you feel? What triggered your emotions? What can you learn from their perspective and how can you approach similar situations in the future with more acceptance and respect?

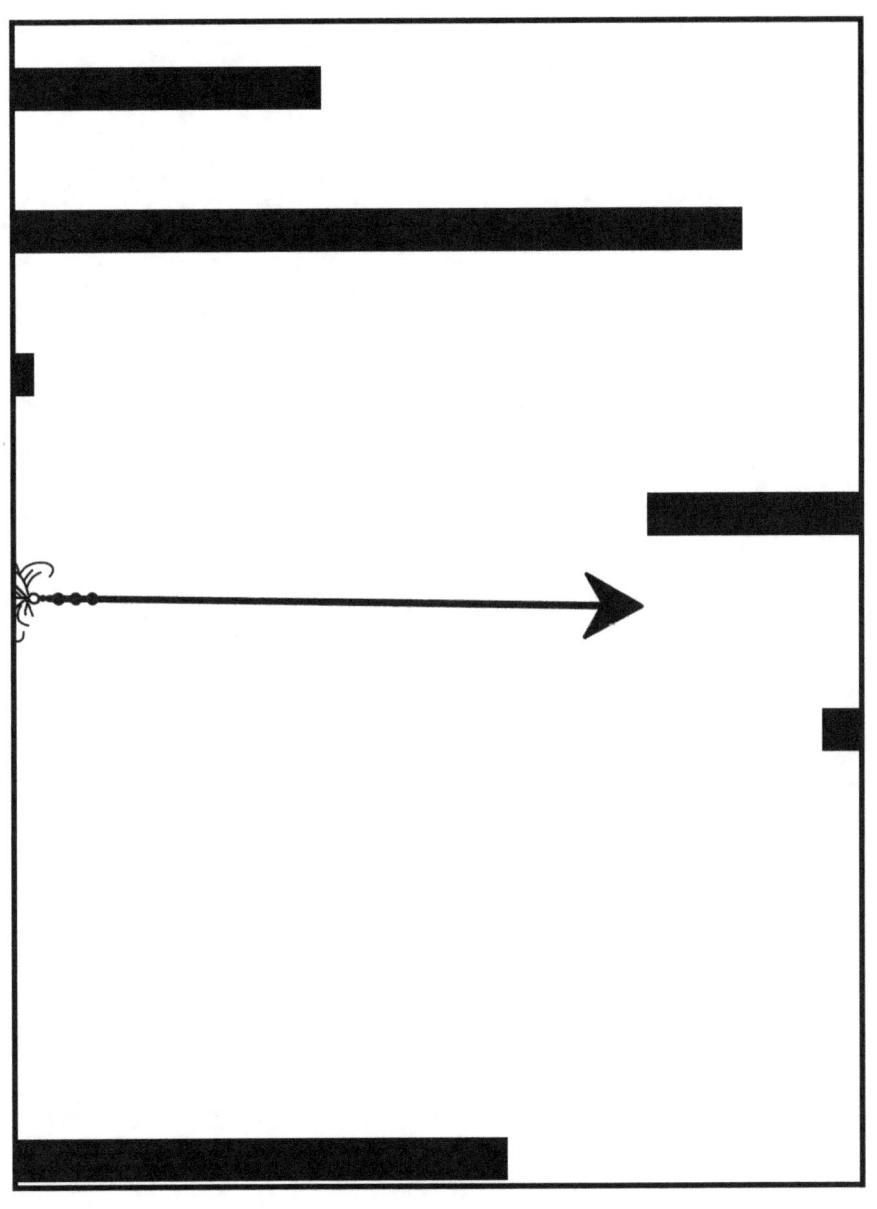

Chapter Twelve

Braver with Belief

Let's recap what we have learned together so far. God will always see us through unexpected circumstances. There is power in letting go of grudges and overcoming regret as we travel the path to forgiveness. As we mended our past hurts, we learned that change isn't something we should fear, but surrender and trust God's direction for us—even if it looks different from what we thought it would. Now, we are kinder to ourselves and have a spirit of gratitude as we work together to be united for a more hopeful future.

I am so proud of all the hard work you've done to get to this point in the book. I know much of this isn't easy to do and likely took you some valuable time in reflection and prayer. You have exercised self-discipline and prioritized your relationship with God over your never ending to-do list, because you see the value in leading in love.

If I had to guess, however, you are still hesitant on your quest to become braver with belief. You may not feel quite ready to exclaim your undying love for the Lord to millions of others. I can't say I blame you— because the times we are in now are proving to be an era of tribulations for Christians who stand up for what and whom they believe in. You may find yourself in the same spot I found myself—too religious for those who don't believe, and not religious enough for the more extreme religious crowd.

Stuck in the Middle

I have always found myself stuck in the middle—of many things. My life has been a series of middle positions: middle child, in the middle of the school cliques, and caught in the middle of political and religious divides. I thought that by being in the middle of everything, I could just escape undetected by others and live my life in a way I wanted. I couldn't have been more wrong.

Being in the middle can be an extremely lonely place as you try to find where you fit the most. The constant desire to be loved and accepted by those in the groups on either side of you may drive you to become someone you wouldn't otherwise be. This can be a dangerous and slippery slope as you become a chronic people-pleaser.

Speaking from experience, I have lost count of the number of times I shifted and bent to do what someone else requested of me, even if it went against my beliefs. It started out small, in a pivot for my stationery business that removed sharing God's Word from the equation. Eventually, however, this shift spilled over into my creative writing process as I attempted to write books in a genre that wasn't suited for me or my beliefs.

The appeal to write a romance book began when I struggled to find books that weren't overly graphic or overboard with the use of foul language. While I can generally handle these in small doses, as my faith deepened, my desire to safeguard my heart and mind would cause me to not finish a book that filled me with spiritual angst.

I began researching the tropes and outline methods used in the making of romance novels to determine how I could create a world that not only was safe for my readers, but also highlighted the importance of God working in and through the relationships of my characters. Because this took quite a bit more time than I expected, I paused the work on my romance series to focus on writing and publishing both *Authentically Anchored*, and now, *Braver with Belief*.

While I would love to tell you that my decision to do this was met with open arms among my peers—I cannot. The disappointment came from friends who weren't used to me being vocal about my beliefs, and they challenged me on the authenticity behind this sudden shift. After sharing what was on my heart, I listened to what was on theirs. Their concerns showed me how much they valued me and our friendship—but lacked an understanding of the reasoning behind my decision.

Countless conversations later, I felt defeated and wanted to give up writing altogether. Should I push my beliefs aside and write what they want me to write, or do I honor God and write what I feel He is asking me to write? Here I was again, stuck in the middle.

The guilt that followed was uncomfortable—and lasted far longer than it should have. I replayed those conversations in my head more times than I care to admit, and even wished I could have just written the book. I don't like disappointing others, which is why I have always been a serial people-pleaser.

The problem, however, arose when I realized that constantly trying to please others was making me unrecognizable to myself. I was miserable. Before long, so were they. No matter how hard I tried to be the person they wanted me to be, I still messed up! By accepting their beliefs, I inadvertently suppressed my own in a misguided attempt to conform. It hadn't occurred to me that acceptance and respect must be mutual.

This realization began to really bother me more with each passing day, as I couldn't shake the feeling that I had relied more on people and less on God. By dampening my belief in God and not leading with a love that showed God in and through me, I separated myself from Him more. While I didn't do it intentionally, moment by moment and choice by choice, people pleasing eventually caught up to me.

Perhaps being in the middle of the road isn't the best place to be, after all. If I can accept others for their beliefs and who they are, couldn't they also accept who I am and what I believe? I wasn't giving them a chance to prove whether this could be true, because I kept quiet about where I stood in my beliefs so as not to offend them.

You will likely come across others who, despite your acceptance of them and their beliefs, will still take offense to you and yours. Not everyone is open-minded with these matters, and the adage of never speaking of politics or religion in social settings has caused us to gloss over really hard conversations that we should have in a controlled and respectful way. Humans are vastly complex, aren't we?

Focus on Pleasing God

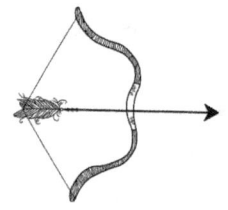

When I think about what it means to be braver with belief, I see myself standing confidently as I share my love for the Lord.

As I share all the goodness He has brought me with someone who may or may not feel the same way that I do, I am completely okay with their response to my testimony.

I know that if there is a harsh judgment, I will have hurt feelings—but I also know their opinion is theirs to have. If it is someone I love and have invited into my life through a relationship, I will listen when they share what is in their hearts. To prevent mirroring hurtful actions, I will respond with love and kindness, showing them God through my actions.

Pleasing others is not why I will attentively listen and lead in love. I do these things because pleasing God is extremely important to me. People-pleasing replaces your reliance on God by putting the expectations of others ahead of the purpose God has intended for you. By trying to always please others, you are clouding your judgment as you intuitively try to listen to your heart. This makes it more difficult to discern the direction God is leading you.

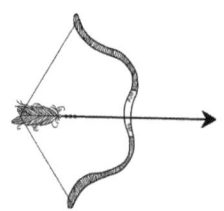

To bravely stand up for what you believe in requires a level of self-discipline deeply rooted and driven only by God's love.

You can still love and accept others while also being brave in your belief and spreading God's message of hope. You can still be in the middle of the road while doing this—and that is completely okay.

I have been cautioned that being a middle-of-the-road Christian is the same as being lukewarm in my faith, but I disagree. By being in the middle of the road, I am relying on God more than ever to discern the truth as I look at what both sides are saying. My faith has grown stronger because I have given myself permission to hear what both sides have to say about a matter before coming to my own conclusions—without agreeing just to please someone else.

I am not afraid to be alone in my belief, either. I know that somewhere out there, there are others who, like me, feel as if they don't belong on either side. If I had to guess, they may not have found a church where they feel welcome, despite trying their best. If you find yourself in this space, my advice to you would be to find a community or group that aligns with your beliefs. If there isn't a community like that for you, create one to fulfill the need. This is how you step out in bravery as a leader, sharing God's love with those around you.

You Are Qualified

In the last chapter, we talked about accepting your calling. Once you obediently say yes to the calling God has placed on your heart, it's time to stop disqualifying yourself so you can walk in faith. So many people disqualify themselves before they allow God the opportunity to work through them. This disbelief is a tactic the enemy uses to keep us from fulfilling what God is calling us to do.

As I consider the past, I think about the ways I have sabotaged myself into believing I wasn't the right person to answer the call. These are things I wish I could have done better—or avoided at all costs—as they have drastically thrown me off the correct path. I pray you learn from my painful mistakes. Sometimes we stand in our own way because we are afraid to fully trust God to do it His way.

Feeling as though I'm not good enough, I believed I lacked the skills, talent, and qualifications needed to be a servant leader. I have had to remind myself many times over that God equips those He calls, not the other way around. The skills and gifts I have are to be used to honor God, not to be hidden away.

My life has been extremely bumpy, and there are many parts of it where I have carried shame. One of the hardest questions I had to ask myself was—why do I feel I must be perfect when I am not Jesus? Putting the high expectation that I need to be perfect in everything I do sets me up for instant failure. If I wait until my creative writing skills are perfected, I may never publish another book. God always uses imperfect people. He wants me to use my experiences to help others get through similar ones they face.

Jesus tells us in Matthew 5:48, *"Be perfect, therefore, as your heavenly Father is perfect."* If you travel back in Matthew and start at verse 43, you'll learn more behind this powerful verse and what He means. It all points us back to loving our enemies. We can take it a step farther when we choose to lead in love in all circumstances. To me, this is the level of perfection I should be striving for.

Comparing myself to others who seem more confident or experienced has also been a major challenge. This was one of the hardest things to release, and ultimately, I had to realize that we are all called to do different things. While they can be similar, our gifts are unique to us. Comparison stops us from forward movement, especially when we really are comparing apples to oranges.

My trifecta of excuses included: I don't have time, I'm not ready yet, and I don't know what I'm doing. It was easy for me to delay my obedience with these excuses.

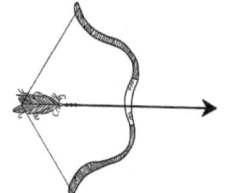

Growth and readiness comes while walking in your calling, not in the preparation.

Don't get hung up on having the perfect plan of action before actually taking action. You really just need that first small step. Everything else will fall into place.

Another thing that tripped me up was believing I was too old, not pretty enough, and too quiet to make a difference. My physical attributes have nothing to do with my calling, neither does my age. These insecurities are things the enemy uses against me because he knows it will cause me to stumble and likely to remain paralyzed in place. Our inaction is his goal. We will not let him win, now will we?

Previous setbacks used to convince me that being a leader was not meant to be. I allowed my failures to determine the outcome before I even tried something new. This thought never occurred to me until recently. Perhaps these setbacks are actually God's way of refining the process to help me get it right.

Don't give up too quickly. Use your setbacks and failures as learning experiences to help you refine the process with God.

The biggest lie of them all that has completely paralyzed me is that nobody sees me and nobody cares. I had to get to the root of the misbelief I carried to determine where that thought came from. The requirement of having an audience on my social media platform was ultimately the source of the misbelief. This is another form of self-sabotage. Impact doesn't require a platform, it only requires obedience. Trust that God will bring the people He wants to come to you in the way He feels is most impactful. Keep showing up, even if you only have one person interacting. That one person may need you more than anyone.

Simply Pray

Ultimately, you should by now have realized that you, my beautiful friend, are more than qualified. The only thing standing between you and fulfilling your calling is obedience. When the day comes that you are face to face with Jesus, He will ask you why you didn't answer His call. How would you answer that question if it came to you today?

That question changed my perspective. Primarily because my first thought was to throw others under the bus, as I explained my reasoning to do everything to please others. I quickly realized, however, this was merely another excuse to make myself feel better for my disobedience. Owning your choice, or lack thereof, is the first step in changing the course you are on.

Consider it a great blessing to have received a calling from God to serve Him. Whether it is by starting a ministry, writing a book, starting a business, applying for a new role, or leading a group, be confident in the choices you make. If you aren't confident about the direction you need to move forward in, take that as your sign to invite God to reveal more to you.

Sometimes, we overcomplicate things to a point where we are distracting ourselves. Pray, friend. Simply pray.

The Unseen Truth

I had to stop trying to please people and start focusing on how I could most please God. This was a tough habit to break, and I still struggle with it from time to time as I find myself back in old patterns. I have a servant's heart and a sense of naivety that often clouds my judgment. I have had to work on addressing self-discipline to become more and more reliant on God as I became less reliant on others.

When you see yourself in the middle of the road, do you lean more towards one side of it rather than standing confidently in your belief? There is nothing wrong with being in the middle of the pack. If the world only had a group of leaders, we may find ourselves in some of the loneliest places as we walk away in our own direction, away from everyone else. By being in the middle, you can become a follower or be a leader of others in the same area as you. That choice is up to you.

If you feel as if you've lost a little of who you are as you have bent and molded to be a version of yourself that someone else likes more, take this as your permission to stop. It's time to become braver with belief as you stand confident in who you are.

When was the last time you did something you felt God leading you to do?

Braver with Belief

*"When I am afraid, I put my trust in you. In God, whose word
I praise—in God I trust and am not afraid. What can mere
mortals do to me?"*

Psalm 56:3-4

In order to become braver with belief, trusting God rather than pleasing people needs to be our default. If you feel afraid of disappointing someone else by simply responding in a way that honors your core values and beliefs, you risk breaking those very values and beliefs that matter most to you. Once I realized I was doing this, I felt like a hypocrite. It was a moment of contention for me as I wrestled with my thoughts on the matter. I honestly thought that by pleasing others, I was not only keeping the peace, but also leading in love. Truthfully, the act of pleasing others left me feeling even more alone than ever before.

If you have to make the choice to either stand up for what you believe in or bend to please someone else, I encourage you to be brave as you confidently express your belief. You can do this in a loving and kind way that honors God and is also respectful of the belief of others. It goes back to the basics of boundaries within your social circles. Set them in place to honor the differences in beliefs you both hold.

Do you feel you rely more on pleasing others or on pleasing God? Be honest with yourself as you reflect on this question to identify any potential places where there is a need for improvement. It's important to note here that you should also forgive yourself for all the times you relied on others instead of God. It's easy to forget how pleasing others can actually take us further from God by removing our reliance on Him. He knows your heart better than anyone else. Allow Him to lead you where you need to go with this.

The Strength in Letting Go

Hiding your faith in God is like taking the bright light within you and putting it inside of a dark box in the back of the closet. If you are afraid to show your faith to others for fear of how they may react, or worry they'll walk away from you forever—have hope and know no matter what happens, God will know and understand your heart. When I am afraid of losing relationships that are important to me, I try to remind myself of the betrayal and persecution Jesus faced. And the fact that despite it all, He still sacrificed His life for yours and mine.

I am not perfect, just like everyone else. Despite my best efforts, I still default to pleasing others first then regretting that decision later. To stop this cycle from continuing, anytime I feel myself bending, I close my eyes and invite Jesus to enter the space with me. This grounds me in the present moment, as I search for His direction and clarity on what to do next.

It's time to let go of the fear of disappointing others. The only thing you need to focus on is your direct connection with God and the relationship the two of you are building. He will take you in the direction you are meant to go. And if He is calling you to it, He most certainly will equip you and see you through it.

What change do you need to make to become braver with belief? Take some time in solitude to consider this question and see what areas come to mind. Journal about anything that comes up; this helps you remember when you face the dilemma of what choice to make in the moment.

Moving Forward with Hope

Becoming braver with belief helps you become stronger and more resilient in your faith. You'll feel closer to God as your connection grows stronger and stronger. Once you've reached this point, you can then work towards serving others. Hearing and answering the call provides direction and clarity. In the next chapter, I will share with you one of my most intimate moments with Jesus, as I say yes to what I feel He is calling me to do.

Braver Choices

Actionable steps you can take to become braver with belief as you step into the role of servant leader. I have broken it down for you in a way that is easier to remember: B.R.A.V.E.R.

Brighten: An action taking call to service to refine our hearts as we discover the area in which to serve.

Serving God: Spend time in solitude. For the first fifteen minutes, pick up your Bible and randomly open it to see what scripture speaks to you on that page. Jot down the scripture reference on a sheet of paper to reflect upon later. Repeat multiple times throughout the fifteen minutes. For the remaining time you choose to be in solitude, spend it in conversation with God. Talk to Him as if He is right beside you. Share what is on your mind and in your heart like you would a friend.

Reflect: A prayer that covers the emotions felt within each chapter with a promise to let go of the things we need to, so we can keep moving forward.

> *Father, I am so sorry that I have put people above you as I bend to please them. Help me let go of being afraid to stand up for what I believe in while dimming the light you shine brightly within. Please forgive me for not relying on you like I should. Amen.*

Act: An action taking exercise that forces us to get up and move forward.

Pick one of the Bible verses that stands out to you from your time in solitude. On a sheet of paper or in your journal, illustrate them with drawings to show the verse in action.

Verse: Memorization of a Bible verse that helps us remember the lesson within the chapter.

Write the following scripture and post it somewhere you'll see it every day; maybe a bathroom mirror, refrigerator, or your home office. Memorize it and refer to it when you need to feel braver.

> *"For the Spirit God gave us does not make us timid, but gives us power, love and self-discipline."*
> 2 Timothy 1:7

Explore: An action taking exercise to help us explore new possibilities we may not have yet thought of.

Exercise: Choose an activity that pushes you outside of your comfort zone, like hiking on a slightly more challenging trail or taking part in a new activity. Once you have selected the activity, get up and do it.

Renew: A journal prompt for us to reflect with God in solitude.

Journal Prompt: Getting outside of my comfort zone made me feel…

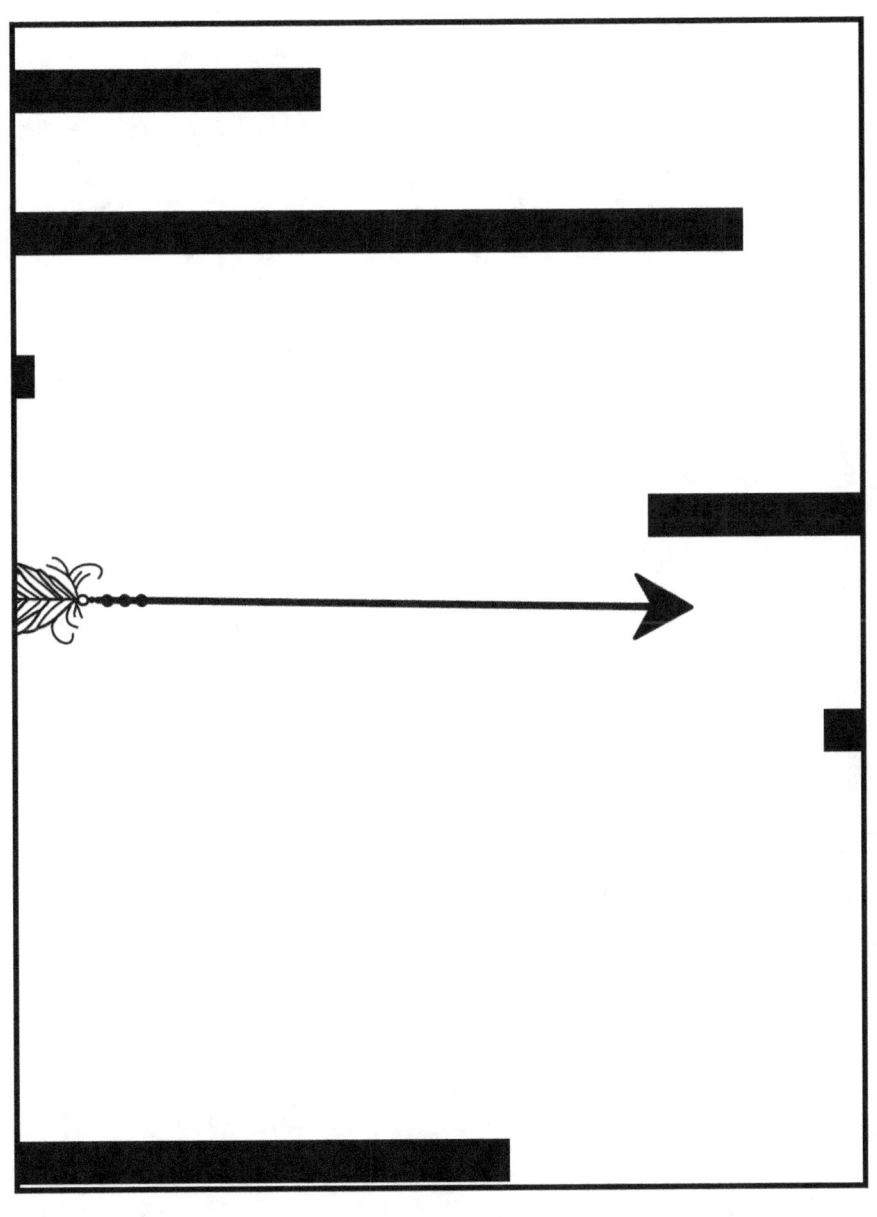

chapter Thirteen

A Sacred Dance

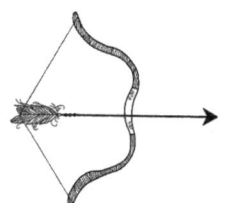

No longer burdened by perfectionism, we find ourselves more purposefully following God's guidance.

It almost feels like a contradiction at first. We want to ensure our actions are pleasing to God, but remembering we aren't perfect gives us the space we need to continue working on aligning ourselves more with God.

Developing good habits through daily solitude with God is excellent, but it's also important to allow God to work according to His timetable. Sometimes, we need to take the backseat with our schedules and ask God to drive us where He wants us to go for the day.

To put this into practice, allow some space within your schedule each day to sit for a moment and ask God to direct you towards what He wants you to do. Your discoveries and subsequent feelings may surprise you.

September 2024 | The Dance

It was an extremely stressful day, causing one of the worst headaches I had in a long time. As I became increasingly frustrated with the complex design I was working on, the colors all began to run together, and my vision became blurry. I sat forward and looked out the window in the distance, trying to refocus my vision as I took a break from the computer screen.

As I concentrated on the treetops, my playlist changed to the next queued up song, filling my office with the sound of strings. I instinctively turned the volume louder despite my headache, leaning back in my chair as I closed my eyes and felt the music moving through me.

Instantly, I found myself in a space facing Jesus, who wore a white robe. His presence alone caused a light so bright it lit up the space all around us. I felt a strong sense of peace and awe as I stood staring at Him. He smiled at me tenderly as He extended His hand.

Curious, I looked at him, my left eyebrow raised as I placed my hand in His in anticipation of what would happen next. As the music picked up, He gently guided me throughout the space, never taking His eyes off of me as we danced to the soothing music. Despite being a terrible dancer in real life, I somehow perfectly kept up with Him, never taking my eyes off of Him.

I could feel myself swaying as I sat in my chair, eyes closed, my hands raised in the same position they were in my vision. I resisted the urge to break the silence by asking Him the millions of questions running through my mind—I simply felt an understanding on His part. The end of the song neared. And I understood so much, even though He hadn't spoken a word.

When the song ended, so did my time spent in the vision with Jesus. I thanked and praised Him in the silence of my office. I quickly pressed pause on my playlist before it had the chance to advance to the next track, allowing myself the time needed to process what I had just experienced. It felt so real, that sacred dance I shared with my Savior; I could feel the love from a Father who loves me.

Suddenly, nothing else seemed to matter. I realized this was an invitation to be more vulnerable with God than I had ever been. I started speaking as if He were beside me in my office. I honestly shared with Him how frustrated I was with my business, and how I felt as if I could and should do more.

With complete authenticity, I conveyed my misery and increasing exhaustion. My firm stance was that changes were necessary to better support my household amidst rising living costs. Surprisingly, I didn't cry. I simply spoke to Him; a conversation between a Father and His daughter.

The process of opening my heart that way to God was an act of vulnerability that led to a deeper connection and a deeper willingness to serve Him. It impacted me more than I had imagined. I heard myself audibly say, "I know you are calling me to serve. And while I don't know how or what to do next, my answer is yes."

Preparations

That moment, I felt the undeniable call to begin serving immediately. The feeling was stronger than any other time I felt led to do something. There was a new sense of urgency, as if the dance was a way to show me I was ready, despite feeling I wasn't. The frustration I had felt earlier was now replaced with peace and joy—and I couldn't help but smile as I kept saying yes repeatedly, in between joyous laughter.

Perhaps this was God's way of getting my attention, reminding me that trusting Him is far more important than anything else I could be doing. Of course, it didn't answer the lingering question of how, what, or who will fund it. I knew, however, that those were things left for me to discover once I aligned myself fully to His will.

I wish I could say that this sacred moment gave me all the answers I needed. It didn't. But—it gave me a piece of the missing puzzle: remembering that each step you take in faith is like a dance, just waiting to be enjoyed. I had forgotten that along the way, as I piled on expectations and timelines that only distracted me from fulfilling my calling. These expectations and timelines replaced the joy I once had with frustration and stress.

Simpler, less hurried times where I could enjoy every moment are what I craved. Although I'm unsure if I'll fully assume my hoped-for role as a woman's retreat organizer, I'm prioritizing time to serve my calling as a woman's ministry leader. I have been saying for years that I wasn't ready and the time wasn't now. After my dance with Jesus, I can hear Him telling me it is time, and I need to begin taking steps to fulfill my calling.

Shortly after this vision, I began reading a book I received as a gift about leading a women's ministry. I have taken my time in each chapter as I put into practice what I am learning to lay the foundation of the ministry I'm called to. By researching an area I felt unqualified in, I could discover all the ways God has been teaching me over the years.

I have also reached out and invited others to join me on a project to fulfill my calling. Because of these steps, *Boldly Woven Magazine* is being created with the intention of weaving our stories together in faith. This ministry is a safe space for multi-passionate women who dare to be different. There is a seat at my table for you to share with others your story of redemption.

As I prepare to enter a season of ministry, I am slowly cutting back what I am doing within my business. This bittersweet decision has been one I haven't taken lightly and has caused many tears to fall. I know that to move into ministry, I need to lighten my load. I am removing services and offerings from my extremely busy plate, exactly as needed. The more I release, the lighter I feel, further reminding me of the dance I had with Jesus. I hope to have the chance to feel that way more often—light, free, and peaceful.

Shifted Focus

One thing is certain: the more in alignment I bring my business to God's plan for me, the more peace enters my heart. Coincidentally, this book has also been extremely timely as well. The Holy Spirit has this remarkable way of guiding me through my projects. When I work with clients, His guidance comes out with messages for their project. Rarely does it ever come out for my projects. As I was working on a romance novel, I felt anxiety creep in as I wrestled with the thought I should work on something else.

The moment I surrendered and allowed myself the freedom to change, to listen to the Holy Spirit, was when I became even more aligned with God's purpose for me. The anxiety disappeared as peace filled its space. The words flew from my fingertips as fast as they entered my mind. Sometimes, God will place a story on your heart for you to share with others who need your guidance. I don't know who needs to hear the stories found within these pages, but I pray this book is helping guide you to discovering your calling.

The incredible thing in all of this is the more I work on what I feel led to work on, the more relaxed I become. If I shift focus onto something else that I want to do—but may not feel called to do—I feel the return of the anxiety as I become more and more unsettled in my decision. I recognize this as God's way of answering my prayer for guidance and direction, and even nudging me in the right direction.

I wrote Chapter Eleven of this book with great focus today, and the words came easily. I could feel God's presence all around me. Further enhancing that feeling, the sun glared through the windows behind me despite the rain that fell from the sky. That feeling has carried me through to this moment. The sun has set, and it is now dark outside. But one thing that remains is God's presence is all around me as I write.

If you are feeling out of alignment and unsure of where to go from here, may I offer this simple reminder? Open your heart to Jesus in a moment of complete vulnerability. Time growing together with the Lord is all you need to recalibrate. It costs nothing but your time, and the payout is far more rewarding. If you want to create a sacred dance with Jesus of your own, take some time today to work through the *Braver Choices* tasks at the end of this chapter.

Go For a Bullseye

With everything I had worked so hard to release from my life, I could now clearly see the importance of connection with God on a deeper level. Over the years, I have developed daily habits to ensure I spend time in solitude with Him every morning. Some days, I may have spent a quick moment in prayer throughout, but most days, morning was my prime time with God.

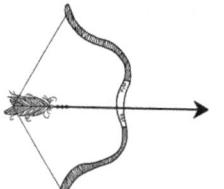

Allowing my schedule to dictate my relationship with God, I found, was a disservice to both of us.

It felt almost as if I was putting God on a shelf as I went about my day with His watchful eye over me—yet not actively engaging with Him. I defended this positioning by justifying it with my schedule. Eventually, however, I realized this was the wrong approach.

It all goes back to the need to control your outcome. We do not have the bigger picture, yet we hastily make decisions without first seeking direction. We have gotten so used to doing it all we feel the need to continue doing it all. This method will undoubtedly end in disappointment.

God didn't create us to do everything alone. We learned this lesson in Genesis when Eve was created to help Adam. In our own stubbornness, we tend to assume far too many responsibilities and refuse help when offered. It is time to take God off the shelf and let Him lead. Trust that He will bring the right people at the right time to relieve the burdens you are carrying.

After my sacred dance, I saw areas where getting help was crucial for survival. Working with a business coach who could help me collect my thoughts and come up with a plan of action that put me back on the right track of answering my calling was the only way I could see a way forward. Admitting my weaknesses in self-sabotage, I needed accountability from someone who would be firm yet loving in their approach. I began praying for a connection with someone who could do this very thing. I began collaborating with others who have gifts in areas I do not, helping to shift my workload.

Consider the areas in your life now that you feel to be lacking. Whether it is lacking direction, clarity, or time—trust God to bring the things you need to move forward again. When overwhelm hits, I am often paralyzed in place, which is why I'm a huge fan of taking action. If I remain paralyzed in place, I tend to run on autopilot. This lack of action leads to a traffic jam of tasks as they continue to pile up until tended to. If I do not jump in and clear the traffic jam, I risk becoming more overwhelmed as the pileup continues to grow due to my inaction.

Taking action ensures we are moving forward towards our goal. It reminds me of a bow and arrow. So, I am asking you to pull the bowstring and arrow back, set your target, say a prayer, and release the arrow, trusting God to guide it exactly where it hits the bullseye.

The Unseen Truth

I had to become vulnerable as I invited Jesus to join me. I have always found it difficult to visualize things I think about. While I have a very vivid and creative imagination, when I close my eyes, I rarely see a scene that matches what I am thinking. I often feel the lack of visibility as proof that what I believe to be true clearly mustn't exist if I cannot see proof that it does. When I closed my eyes and listened to the music that day, it was the first time I could visually see the scene unfolding as if I were truly there.

Can you lay everything down to be more vulnerable as you invite Jesus to join you in a dance? My sacred dance has filled me with a hope so strong that it propels my daily decisions to ensure I'm in alignment with God's will for my life in this season. If I get stuck deciding what I should do next, I simply close my eyes, invite Jesus to join me, and sit in silence until I feel a shift. I notice how the thoughts I have make me feel. If I get goosebumps, this is my way of identifying guidance from the Holy Spirit. Your sense of Holy Spirit leading may look or feel different. If I get knots in my stomach, I know I need to keep thinking, as following peace is always the way to go.

How the Spirit moves us is unique to each of us. The closer to God you become, the more you'll begin to feel and see Him at work in your life. If you feel a call to serve, do not be afraid of your decision to accept that call. Trust that God will equip you to serve as you bravely step out in faith to share His love with others.

Are you ready to bravely move forward in faith?

Braver with Belief

> *"You turned my wailing into dancing; you removed my sackcloth and clothed me with joy, that my heart may sing your praises and not be silent. LORD my God, I will praise you forever."*
> Psalm 30:11-12

In order to become braver with belief, simply surrendering and trusting isn't enough. Lay aside everything as you invite Jesus to join you in the space you are and become more vulnerable with Him. Your vulnerability forms a deeper connection with God, removing feelings of uncertainty and replacing them with joy.

He calls us all to do different and various things to glorify His kingdom. Do not be afraid of what you feel He is calling you toward, but pray for guidance and wisdom to help prepare you as you say yes to serving others. As you are more vulnerable with Him, pray for wisdom and guidance to help equip you as you lead.

Where do you feel God guiding you now? Perhaps it is to volunteer at your church to help in an area that needs you. Maybe it is to lead a new ministry to help others in a way that only you can. It could be that He is asking you to share your testimony by writing a book. No matter what the call is, be brave and confidently say yes. The rest will fall into place as you follow Him.

The Strength in Letting Go

Prior to my dance, I held on to my life so tightly my knuckles were white. Serving was my desire, but what if I failed? How could I fund a ministry I wanted to start? Although I was unsure of the answers to two important questions, clinging to my current situation to secure my income stalled my progress.

I could feel the tension rising within my body the more I fought it. It wasn't until I let go of the grip of control, I could see more clearly the need to go where I was being led. Each step in my faith is like a dance. I am guided by Jesus as He leads me closer and closer to fulfilling my purpose. I know He will do the same for you.

It's time to let go of the grip you are trying to have on your life and allow God to guide you where He needs you. Once you stop fighting this change within you, you'll feel more at peace as you step into fulfilling your purpose in life. The more you continue to fight it, however, the harder it will be to discover exactly what your purpose is.

What do you feel God calling you to do—and are you ready to answer His call? Have a conversation with Him. Be completely vulnerable, honest, and real with Him. He already knows your thoughts before you speak a single word, therefore, do not hold back anything. Write down anything that comes to mind during your time with Him; the answer can likely be found there.

Moving Forward with Hope

It is important to be receptive to His guidance. In allowing God the chance to work in and through you, your intentions and actions will change to be more in alignment with Him. Once you are ready, fully let go of all that you are clinging to as you say yes to what awaits you. You are about to enter a season of new beginnings, which is exactly what we will cover in the next chapter.

Braver Choices

Actionable steps you can take to become braver with belief as you step into the role of servant leader. I have broken it down for you in a way that is easier to remember: B.R.A.V.E.R.

Brighten: An action taking call to service to refine our hearts as we discover the area in which to serve.

Serving God: Play this song as you spend time alone with Jesus. Stand up, close your eyes, and dance with Jesus as the music plays. Keep your mind quiet as you focus on visualizing your dance with Jesus. Don't speak, don't think, just dance.

Shepherd (Hotel Sessions)
by Local Sound

Reflect: A prayer that covers the emotions felt within each chapter with a promise to let go of the things we need to, so we can keep moving forward.

> *Father, I am so sorry for clinging too tightly to my life. Help me let go fully as I trust more in you. Please forgive me for continually telling you I wasn't ready when you kept showing me I was. Amen.*

Act: An action taking exercise that forces us to get up and move forward.

Mind Map: Start with the center circle and write "Serving Others" inside. Branch out into specific actions, groups of people, areas of need, etc. Brainstorm as many ideas as you can come up with. Once completed, spend time in prayer seeking wisdom and direction. Keep coming back to your list until you know which direction you are called to go.

Verse: Memorization of a Bible verse that helps us remember the lesson within the chapter.

Write the following scripture and post it somewhere you'll see it every day; it's a bathroom mirror, refrigerator, or your home office. Memorize it and refer to it when you struggle with saying yes.

"Then I heard the voice of the LORD saying, 'Whom shall I send? And who will go for us?' And I said, 'Here am I. Send me!'"
Isaiah 6:8

Explore: An action taking exercise to help us explore new possibilities we may not have yet thought of.

Exercise: Take part in a community service project or other charity work that aligns with your mind map. Volunteer to help, spend time in that element. When finished, write in your journal about how your service connects to your purpose and calling.

Renew: A journal prompt for us to reflect with God in solitude.

Journal Prompt: Is there an area where you feel called to serve? If yes, what steps can you take to answer this call more fully? If not, what areas on your mind map do you feel most drawn to and why?

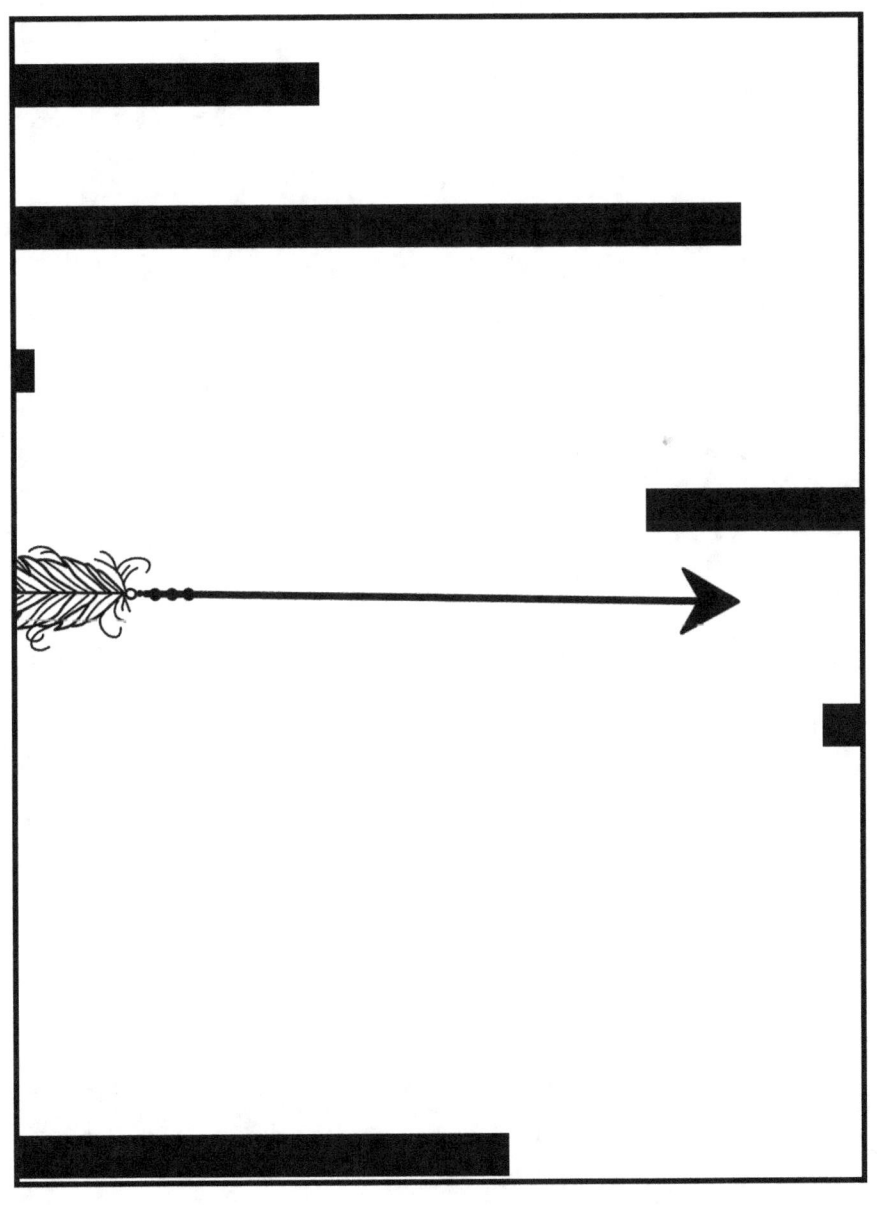

chapter Fourteen

New Beginnings

Getting our rhythm back in timing with God's is precisely the thing we needed to bring us to our next big step: a new beginning. Now, finding the strength to start encourages us rather than causing us to fear.

This is great in theory. But we are human, and human nature is to wrestle with our decision to change. We tend to over-analyze the many things that could go wrong instead of dreaming about what could go right.

The time you spend in transitioning to a new beginning varies from person to person. Sometimes, right as you step into your new role, a setback occurs and you find yourself back where you once were. Don't give up. This is merely a test of your commitment to God and His plans for you.

December 2024 | God's Perfect Timing

The familiar feeling of self-awareness paired with discernment when making decisions returned. It was a subtle shift at first. But the more I acknowledged what I was feeling, the stronger discernment grew. After my sacred dance, I quickly realized that who I am shifted as it matched the alignment already initiated by saying yes. Six months have now passed from the moment of the dance to today—the day I am writing this chapter—which coincides with the ending of the year.

This time of year, you may hear people telling you all the changes you need to make as you vow that the new year will bring a new you. It should be no surprise to you, however, that most New Year's resolutions fail before the end of January arrives. When you are reading this chapter, it may not even be close to the start of the new year—and you may be wondering where I am going with this topic. Stay with me. I promise I will help you understand the importance of this moment.

Before we get there, however, let's go back to a recent moment when I decided writing this book had to be done. I felt strongly that God was calling me to it. As I plotted out what each chapter would hold, I admitted to two very close friends how concerned I was about reaching this point of the book. I wasn't sure I had fully learned the life lesson I hoped to share in this chapter. In my conversation, I asked my friends how I could write about something I hadn't fully lived through yet. I half expected them to tell me to skip writing it. The easy way out, right?

My friends didn't let me quit. Instead of telling me not to write about it, they encouraged me to look at it from a different angle. I prayed every time I sat down to write as my way of inviting God to join me in what is being said. As I stared at the blank screen before me and glanced at my notes to begin this chapter with exactly where I am currently, I struggled with the irony of the timing.

Long ago, I avoided making resolutions at the start of the new year, knowing I'd never follow through. Instead, I adopted viewing my birthday as the trigger point for a new chapter in my life to begin. My birthday is in late September, and every year at this time, I pick a new focus to help fuel my personal growth. I consciously use a word of the year to remind myself to be intentional in my daily interactions by exuding the very definition of the word selected for that year. Words like joy, peace, anchored, resilient, and fellowship have all been integral to shaping me into the woman I am today.

What I love about viewing resolutions like this is that the expectation I will be successful at upholding a resolution that normally wouldn't fit within my lifestyle is removed. Then I can put my energy into seeing how many ways I can incorporate my new focus word into my life before my next birthday. To reiterate this concept, my word for chapter 46 of my life is *fellowship*. I am now three months into it and can proudly tell you about all the amazing opportunities for fellowship I have had over this short timeframe.

Are you curious how much of a challenge fellowship could be for me as an introvert, when it is so natural for others? Therein lies the beauty of this concept. As I shared earlier, I've enjoyed solitude for the past several years and prefer staying home to socializing. Crowded places quickly drain me because I absorb the energies of those around me. A quiet room, alone, is where I feel most like myself—much more than being around others.

Picking "fellowship" as my focus forces me to step way outside of my comfort zone as I began saying yes to invitations to gather with others. I have found a gentle reminder in these invitations about the importance and scarcity of time. I crave the connections I am strengthening with my friends and family, as I also consider the realities of difficult life circumstances we are currently facing. I've adopted a completely new way of thinking. This shift in thinking is unlike anything I've ever known, yet I approached this realistic realization positively.

Could it be possible I am entering a new beginning of my own, as my heart shifts into new territories that soften me in ways I never expected? Perhaps this is because I am growing wiser with age. However, I believe this change is happening in part to obediently saying yes to serving God. I have wrestled with this decision for many years—27 to be exact. It makes me wonder why I never prioritized my relationship with God before now, despite claiming to love and honor him.

Maybe it is in part to God's perfect timing of the approaching new year and writing a chapter on new beginnings. Or maybe this is His way of getting my attention by showing me the humor in the situation, because He knows I will notice it. Either way, today has been a day I struggled to open my laptop and write. I have been procrastinating in ways that had me thinking about what I want to do in the new year for my business.

Spoiler alert! I still don't know exactly what I am going to do next year, but I know the approach I'm taking feels right. A growing desire has been to slow down, make purposeful choices, and reduce my expectations—all while simplifying my life. Practicing this approach has resulted in more peace, better sleep, and overflowing joy.

Don't Be Afraid

Fear of the end of my stationery brand has caused me to avoid needed changes in my business. What I realized, however, is this could actually be the beginning of something new and incredible. If I continue to fear the change awaiting me while holding onto control of a situation, that is a disservice to both me and God. Missing out will lead to regret later on. I admit, change is scary. The fear of completely changing everything I've known for the last eight years is real, and I won't sugarcoat it.

Let's look at this from a different angle. I have also been avoiding changing my lack of exercise routine, hoping to bring it more into alignment with my current nutrition changes and needs. Perhaps what I fear in this situation is the time spent exercising will take from my time spent somewhere else, resulting in a stressful time-shift situation. Allowing my fear of time changes keeps me from doing an activity that further enhances my overall health and wellbeing is actually sabotaging my goal of becoming healthier.

Fear of change can likely apply to the new beginning that awaits you. When we say yes to serving God, a shift in our current actions or schedules may need to happen to free up our time to fulfill the commitment we just made to God. When we realize exactly what is shifting, vulnerability may set in, and our excuses to not move forward keep us stuck in the same place. Try to look at your yes as a way to wipe the slate clean—to start fresh with a completely different perspective, ideas, and goals.

But remember: just because you said yes doesn't mean God will give you every single answer you need to move forward. You can learn precious lessons from discovering the steps you will take. You can then pass these lessons on to others you encounter in life. It's a full-circle moment when your life lesson becomes the answer to help someone through theirs. There is no greater act of service than to share your vulnerabilities, intending to help others who are struggling.

If you are in a similar place as I am right now, I would encourage you to keep seeking the answers you desire. Pray diligently, study daily, and be open to receiving signs from God in unexpected places.

I believe it was not a coincidence as I was scrolling on my phone today. A video played—with a timely message at the exact moment I needed it. The video prompted an action I need to do more—I turned off my phone to write ideas that surfaced—ultimately gave me the answer I had been seeking.

Depend on God

New beginnings are full of energy, possibilities, and a gentle whisper from God, reminding you that this is your time. You shift your mindset from one that focuses on the chaos that comes with not knowing what to do next, to focusing on what you know is the right thing to do now. Change happens when you stop fighting all you've been through and start focusing on the new things ahead.

You see things with a fresh perspective. What once felt stuck or heavy now feels light, hopeful, and full of opportunities. Much like spring, the feeling of new growth becomes exciting as you dream again.

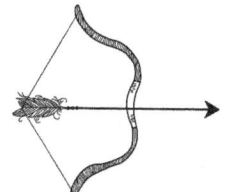

The more you depend on God, the more clarity you have.

Your priorities shift, and you feel more focused on intentional living as you align yourself with God's purpose for you. As you realign, you start to naturally release the things that no longer serve you to make room for healing and growth.

The more you let go of the things that are holding you back, you'll feel the release of the shackle that held you in place, allowing you to leap forward. This new perspective builds a fire in your heart that breathes new life inside of you. It helps you feel alive and full of purpose.

Once that fire is lit again, you'll want to keep it growing so you can share it with others whose fire has grown cold. They need you to help breathe this new life into them, to share with them all the goodness God has for them.

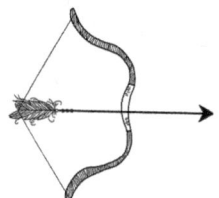 **This new beginning you face is the start of a revival.**

The Unseen Truth

I recognized a change within as I started paying attention to my daily actions, thoughts, and mindset. This level of self-awareness helped me to think clearly, as I took action to make plans for my new beginnings. Inviting God to join me opened up my heart to fully understand the meaning within the message of authenticity and servant leadership He has placed on my heart. Having a strong desire to fulfill my promise to God when I said yes to serving, I feel a sense of urgency to make sure every facet of my business and life are in complete alignment to my calling.

Close your eyes and consider your actions today. Can you pinpoint areas where your actions either were or were not in alignment with your calling? For those that were, why do you think it came so naturally for you to make those choices? For those that were not, what could you do differently next time to ensure they are more in alignment? When you consider these areas, it is common for you to feel a shift or sense of urgency to change what you are doing and how you are doing it. I have always felt this is God's way of showing me how the Spirit works in and through me as I lay down my old ways to pick up the new ones He is guiding me towards.

Your new beginning doesn't have to wait until the new year or your birthday. It can begin right now. Each new day is a chance for a new beginning to help you achieve your goal of fulfilling your purpose.

Are you ready to wipe the slate clean and start fresh?

Braver with Belief

"Therefore, if anyone is in Christ, the new creation has come: The old has gone, the new is here!"
2 Corinthians 5:17

In order to become braver with belief, we must let go of the old before we can celebrate the new. Prior to saying yes, it is possible we struggled with a negative mindset—why on earth would we want to help people when they were cruel to us or let us down? How can I help others when my life has been filled with hardships I have had to overcome on my own? Eventually, these questions hardened our hearts, causing us to stop serving others. We removed this old way of thinking the moment we said "yes" to serving.

The new experiences that await you now can be both frightening and exciting all at once. Remember where fear comes from; it is often a tactic used to keep you from making forward progress for the good of the Lord. Hold on to the excitement and joy you feel when you think of the possibilities before you.

What change do you feel you need now—to let go of the old and welcome the new? Spend some time considering this question as it correlates to what your yes is. For example, if your yes is to serve by starting a business, the first change you need to make could be to ensure all that you are planning to do is in alignment with the big goal of launching a new business. If your yes is to share your testimony by writing a book, the first change you need to make could be to seek guidance from the Holy Spirit as you outline your story. If your yes is to start a ministry that serves others, the first change you need to make could be to determine who your ministry will serve.

The Strength in Letting Go

Sitting in this same chair, I am a completely different person than who I was a year ago. The level of growth I have seen within myself went unnoticed for most of the year. It wasn't until recently I realized how substantial of a shift actually occurred this year. This is a good thing, as it showed me the areas in which I opened myself up within my relationship with God and followed His lead more than my own. The absence of stress and anxiety is another sign of proper choices across the vast spectrum of changes made this year on my journey to better health.

Once I changed my eating habits, my approach to business, and my intention to serve, the next logical thing for me to do was take action towards those changes. In the beginning, I would beg God to give me direction—while sitting and waiting. This resulted in frustration when nothing would happen, as I remained fixated in place. Eventually, I woke up and realized the only way I would see a transformation was by taking the steps to make it happen, beginning with inviting God to join me.

It's time to let go of waiting for direction and opening your eyes to discovering the small signs from Him around you. Once you've wiped the slate clean and stepped out in faith, you no longer need to try and control your next steps as you move forward. Inviting God to join you in conversation as you begin your new direction will open your heart in ways you've likely never experienced before, or perhaps haven't in a long time.

Thinking back to the change you uncovered in the last section, what first step must you take to become the catalyst for this change? Schedule the actions needed to fulfill this first step within your schedule and invite God to join you as, together, you get started.

Moving Forward with Hope

Together, we are finally letting go of fear as we fill its place with excitement for what is yet to come. You have worked so hard to get to this point in your life. Slow down a bit to enjoy every moment along the way. Be brave in your change as you step out into this new beginning with a humble heart. It is so easy to fall into the trap of seeking recognition on the road to service, which is why in the next chapter, we are going to take a closer look at this very topic.

Braver Choices

Actionable steps you can take to become braver with belief as you step into the role of servant leader. I have broken it down for you in a way that is easier to remember: B.R.A.V.E.R.

Brighten: An action taking call to service to refine our hearts as we discover the area in which to serve.

Serving Others: You pick who and how you are going to serve. Make sure the choice you make is in alignment with God and the yes you said that started your new beginnings.

Reflect: A prayer that covers the emotions felt within each chapter with a promise to let go of the things we need to, so we can keep moving forward.

> *Father, I am so sorry for not inviting you to sit with me every time I work towards creating a future in serving you. Help me let go of waiting on Your direction and start inviting You to open my heart to see the signs You've lovingly placed around me. Please forgive me for thinking I could do all of this on my own. I need You now more than ever before. Amen.*

Act: An action taking exercise that forces us to get up and move forward.

Spend time in prayer and journal about your new beginning to serve. Ask for guidance from God on how to take the first step, and write everything that comes to mind after you ask and commit to your plan. Write any other thoughts or inspirations that come during your time spent in prayer.

Verse: Memorization of a Bible verse that helps us remember the lesson within the chapter.

Write the following scripture and post it somewhere you'll see it every day, maybe it's a bathroom mirror, refrigerator, or your home office. Memorize it and refer to it when you face a new beginning.

> *"He who was seated on the throne said, 'I am making everything new!' Then he said, 'Write this down, for these words are trustworthy and true.'"*
>
> Revelation 21:5

Explore: An action taking exercise to help us explore new possibilities we may not have yet thought of.

Exercise: Write out your plan to serve. Whether it's volunteering at your church or a local organization, starting a ministry, or caring for a family member. No matter what you feel led to do, know that you are doing good in the world, and honoring God with your obedience. Include in your plan who you plan to serve, how you plan to serve them, and why you are planning to serve.

Renew: A journal prompt for us to reflect with God in solitude.

Journal Prompt: How can I make time in my life to focus on serving, and how will I balance it with my other commitments?

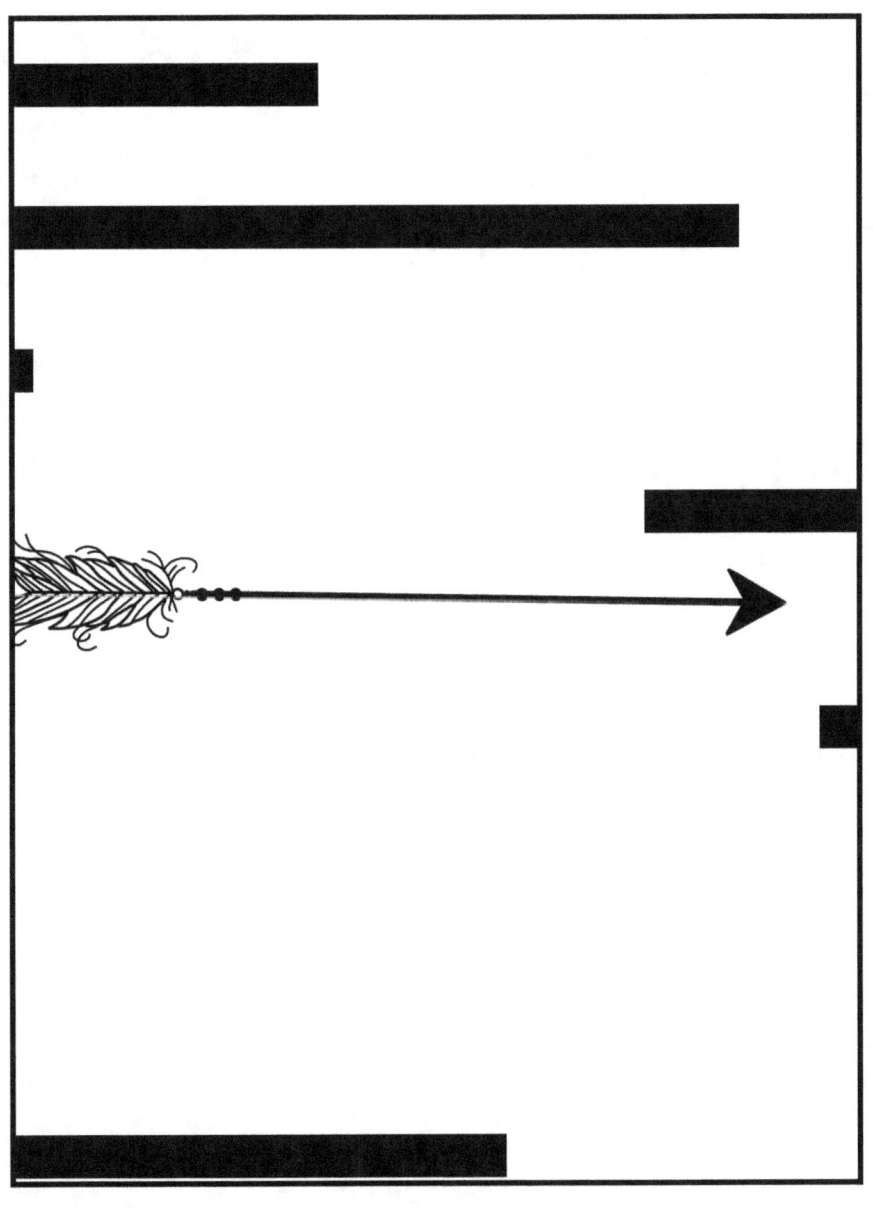

Chapter Fifteen

A Humble Heart

The excitement of a new beginning is invigorating with the promises it carries. It's easy to be so completely focused on what lies ahead that we cannot see what is right beside us in the "now." As our excitement builds, we may overshare our plans with close friends or family too soon. Though unintentional, this may come across as boastful to someone who questions your sudden transformation.

This can be dangerous territory. We don't want to put out the fire burning within you; rather, add kindling to it to keep it growing—always with a humble heart. It is important to always give God glory by acknowledging that He is the source of your strength, creativity, and opportunities.

Resist the temptation to prematurely over share your plans. Safeguard them until the right time comes. Pray for discernment as you reveal all you have been working on. Let your work and character speak as you lead by example in quiet confidence. This shows proof that God is working in and through you as you lay the foundation of what's to come.

Hard Lessons in Humility

The new year finally arrived. As we turned the page to welcome 2025, I felt hopeful. Despite this newfound feeling of hope, I found myself struggling with starting my annual business planning. The clarity needed for me to enter my new beginning was still missing. After not taking much of a break over the holidays, I found my client roster overbooked for the beginning of the year. I prayed for more time to spend in solitude with God.

It was the weekend of January 4th, and I was on the phone with my mom while also getting ready to vacuum the floors. I picked up my stick vacuum to carry it to the front of the house, when suddenly, a sharp electrical-like feeling went through my arm, all the way from my thumb to my elbow. I lost my grip and dropped the vacuum, sending it crashing to the floor.

At first, I shook it off as a fluke occurrence. However, over the next week, pain persisted in my elbow and the feeling and grip in my hand never returned. Stress and worry took root when I realized that something wasn't right with my arm. It became increasingly difficult to work, as I couldn't use the mouse on my computer anymore. Putting my pride aside, I made an appointment to be seen by an orthopedic specialist to determine the cause.

After testing and examination by two surgeons, I learned surgery was my only option to regain mobility and feeling. Although the diagnosis was both carpal and cubital tunnel syndrome, the results of my tests were promising. It sounded like a simple procedure—however, there was a possibility once they got started, this could change. The surgeon couldn't promise me a timeline for recovery, which worried me considering client work. I requested to postpone the surgery by one month, allowing me the chance to finish all the outstanding jobs on my docket.

This proved to be a costly decision. As more time passed, the worse my prognosis became, slowing me down with decreased mobility. The day before surgery, I submitted files to my last client mere minutes before leaving for pre-operative testing. I was grateful, however, for having cleared my schedule, which would allow a month of healing after surgery.

On the day of surgery, I was surprisingly calm. I had a knowing and understanding that God was with me and everything would turn out okay. Two days after surgery, however, was an entirely different story. As the nerve block wore off, the severity of the pain became clear. Due to my digestive issues, I couldn't take medication to help with pain and swelling. The lack of medication intervention only exacerbated my swelling and pain.

They always tell you with any surgery, day three is the worst. And it certainly was. I sat in my recliner, tears streaming down my face as I cried in agony. All I could do was pray. I asked God to help me get through the pain and never leave my side. Going through recovery this way reminded me that God doesn't always take away our pain—but He never leaves us as we are experiencing it. My pain and swelling were so intense, I barely slept those first two weeks.

To make matters worse, I was no longer independent. To rely on Mike for help with daily tasks such as bathing and dressing was a real life lesson in humility. He has seen me during some really grim moments, however, we had experienced nothing like this before. It was extremely hard on both of us. The added responsibility of caring for me was taxing on Mike, and the lack of control of my situation made me feel utterly helpless.

Neither of us understood why I was struggling to the extent I was. It didn't line up with what the surgeon had told us prior to surgery to expect during recovery. Something was off. My doctor instructed me to attend physical therapy when I went for stitch removal.

At my therapy consult appointment—exactly three weeks after surgery—my therapist seemed a bit frazzled as he read my chart. Curious, I inquired to find out what was wrong. I was shocked to discover that my simple procedure had been much more complex than originally believed. This was news to me, as no one had mentioned it until now.

The sound in the room disappeared as I felt a wave of nausea come across me. Missing most of what he had said to me, I snapped out of it when I heard him tell me he couldn't help me. Hearing that I needed a therapist who specialized in fine motor skills caused my heart to race. This wasn't the plan we had agreed to when I said yes to surgery. Instead, this was the worst-case scenario I didn't believe would happen to me.

After I returned home from the therapy consultation, emotions overwhelmed me as I collapsed into a chair at the kitchen table. Unable to hold it in anymore, I sobbed. The chances of me fully regaining the use of my arm had been drastically reduced, just like that. I didn't know if I could ever design again.

The Struggle

As I tried to process the overwhelming emotions, I had a moment where my thoughts were competing with themselves. Taking to prayer, I bluntly asked God what the purpose of all of this was. I recalled a time when I jokingly told Him that He would have to take my right arm to get me to make a drastic change in my business. Obviously, I didn't mean it. But I would never joke like that again, as I literally cannot use my right arm now. Not knowing if I could ever do something I am extremely passionate about filled me with worry. If not design, then what?

As I am writing this chapter, it has now been six weeks post surgery. Writing about the day I found out about the complexity of my surgery immediately brought those emotions back. Looking back at all I have endured these last six weeks, I can confidently say that through it all, God has never left my side. He let me crawl up in His lap and lay my head down as I wept day after day. I poured out all of my brokenness in a way I have never been able to before.

This season of healing, as I called it, opened my heart to things I had buried so deeply. God answered my prayer for more time in solitude. Of that, I was absolutely certain. Just when I didn't think I could change anymore, He surprised me with a few more lessons in humility, trust, and patience.

There were days I would tell God I didn't have the strength to process what He was asking me to walk through. Yet somehow, on those days, He helped me have the most powerful breakthroughs.

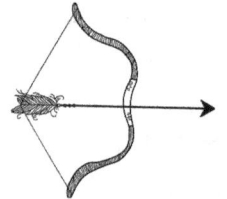

When we agree to serve God, we must go through a refining of our heart and spirit to prepare us for what comes next.

This refining process will push us to our breaking point to see if we will keep going beyond it. It is during this time that we put our full reliance on God and put our pride aside.

Be God's Messenger

Having a humble heart means different things—willingness to serve without recognition, valuing others, or even approaching life with a mindset of growth. It's thinking of yourself less and others more by exercising active listening with a closed mouth and an open heart. As you listen to them, allow God to guide your actions, decisions, and the conversation you have.

Sometimes things come up to you so you can share with a person in need. This is what it means to be a messenger of God; sharing what He places on your heart with those He has brought to you.

By being silent and simply listening, you become present as you take in everything being discussed. Thoughts may flood in, which can make it difficult to discern what God wants you to share with that person. Share from your heart in a way that encourages and uplifts. When someone is hurting, they don't come to you looking for you to fix the problem; they simply need hope. Give them hope by sharing God's Word with them.

During those first few weeks after surgery, I felt like all hope was gone—especially once I found out my recovery would now be far longer than ever imagined. I had to understand the boundaries within my physical limitations and allow others to care for me. Being an extremely private person, I only shared my struggles with a few close friends and family members.

By being vulnerable in sharing my struggles with them, I gave others the opportunity to use their gifts to serve me. This taught me I don't always have to be so strong that I carry the brunt of the weight. Allowing grace to cover what I can't, will give room for God to use others in unexpected ways. I learned there are many messengers for God who come to you when you need them the most.

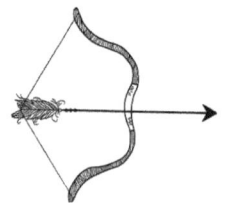

As you become a servant leader, may you move forward with a humble heart, celebrating those whose lives you are changing for the glory of the Lord.

The Unseen Truth

I experienced humility in several instances. God humbled me by showing me I couldn't do everything on my own and needed help from others.

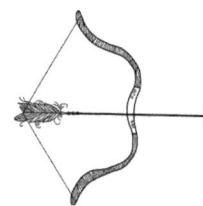

He also taught me healing is holy work that requires patience, trust, and surrender.

Humility is opening our hearts to the possibility of serving without recognition for the sake of making a difference. If we do something because we expect to gain something in return, we are not doing it for the glory of God—but for our own glory. Our actions—whether good or otherwise—can be seen by others. It is imperative for us to be mindful of our actions and how they may impact others.

Allow God to use you to be His messenger to those who need you. By surrendering to Him in this way, you may prepare your heart to help lead a conversation that instills hope to someone who feels hopeless.

What would it look like to serve quietly?

Braver with Belief

"Do nothing out of selfish ambition or vain conceit. Rather, in humility value others above yourselves."
Philippians 2:3

In order to become braver with belief, we must step aside and allow God to lead. It may be challenging to take on a more silent role when we are used to being in the spotlight. However, by valuing others above yourself, you are exemplifying what it means to lead in humility and love.

Leading authentically shows others you can be a safe space to rely on during their time of need. Ask God to prepare your heart continually as you humbly lead those He brings into your life. In their time of struggle, it is important to put aside thoughts focused on yourself so you can serve them well. Learning how to discern what to say and when to say it takes time and practice. Be patient as you work through this and seek God's direction first.

Are you willing to lead the way Jesus did, even if it costs you? This is a question to consider before becoming a servant leader. Ultimately, Jesus paid the highest price by being crucified. By living a godly life, we risk being persecuted for our belief in Jesus and leading in a God-centered manner. Prepare your heart to lead humbly in a way that honors Him.

The Strength in Letting Go

Through everything I have experienced with my carpal tunnel and ulnar nerve transposition surgery, I have learned to be silent in order to engage in active listening. I enjoy talking, so I'll be the first to admit I haven't always been the greatest in ceasing to talk long enough for someone else to join in the conversation.

My friend, it's time to let go of the need to always be the one talking and start practicing active listening. Sometimes all someone needs is for you to listen so they feel heard. Don't feel you have to fix anyone or any situation they are in. Having a humble heart means you are supporting others in a way that lifts them up and encourages them to keep going.

What would change in your life if you led more from a place of humility? Consider the possibility of connecting with others more deeply as you lend a helping hand.

Moving Forward with Hope

A humble heart recognizes the gifts God has given you; blessings from Him and not solely the result of your personal effort. Give thanks for the gifts He's given you to share with others. Don't hide your gifts. Use them in a way that honors God. Putting them to use helps you become a servant leader, which is what we will discuss in the final chapter.

Braver Choices

Actionable steps you can take to become braver with belief as you step into the role of servant leader. I have broken it down for you in a way that is easier to remember: B.R.A.V.E.R.

Brighten: An action taking call to service to refine our hearts as we discover the area in which to serve.

Serving Others: Reach out to a trusted friend and ask if you can practice active listening. Before starting, be sure to explain to your friend that they will need to share a story, thoughts, or struggles while you work on actively listening. Prior to beginning, encourage them to change stories midway and see if you can catch it and keep up. At the end of their story, repeat back everything you remembered and see how close you are—or not. This will show you where your strengths and weaknesses are when listening.

Reflect: A prayer that covers the emotions felt within each chapter with a promise to let go of the things we need to, so we can keep moving forward.

> *Father, I am so sorry for not always giving you the glory as I sought recognition. Help me let go of the need to always be the one talking and start practicing active listening. Please forgive me for not using my gifts to their fullest potential. I desire to always serve with a humble heart. Amen.*

Act: An action taking exercise that forces us to get up and move forward.

Spend time in solitude. Ask God to reveal areas where you may need to humble yourself or let go of pride. After your time in prayer, look up and study verses on humility. Make note of any you find to memorize. End your time in prayer, ask for strength to live with a humble heart, and give gratitude for what you've already learned during your time in solitude.

Verse: Memorization of a Bible verse that helps us remember the lesson within the chapter.

Write the following scripture and post it somewhere you'll see it every day, maybe it's a bathroom mirror, refrigerator, or your home office. Memorize it and refer to it when you struggle to have a humble heart.

"Humble yourselves, therefore, under God's mighty hand, that he may lift you up in due time."
1 Peter 5:6

Explore: An action taking exercise to help us explore new possibilities we may not have yet thought of.

Exercise: Pick three people you can encourage. Write a letter to each of them with what you admire or appreciate about them. Be specific about the qualities and why you are expressing gratitude to them. Mail them the letters and/or cards.

Renew: A journal prompt for us to reflect with God in solitude.

Journal Prompt: How can I work on letting go of pride or the need for praise in my daily interactions with others?

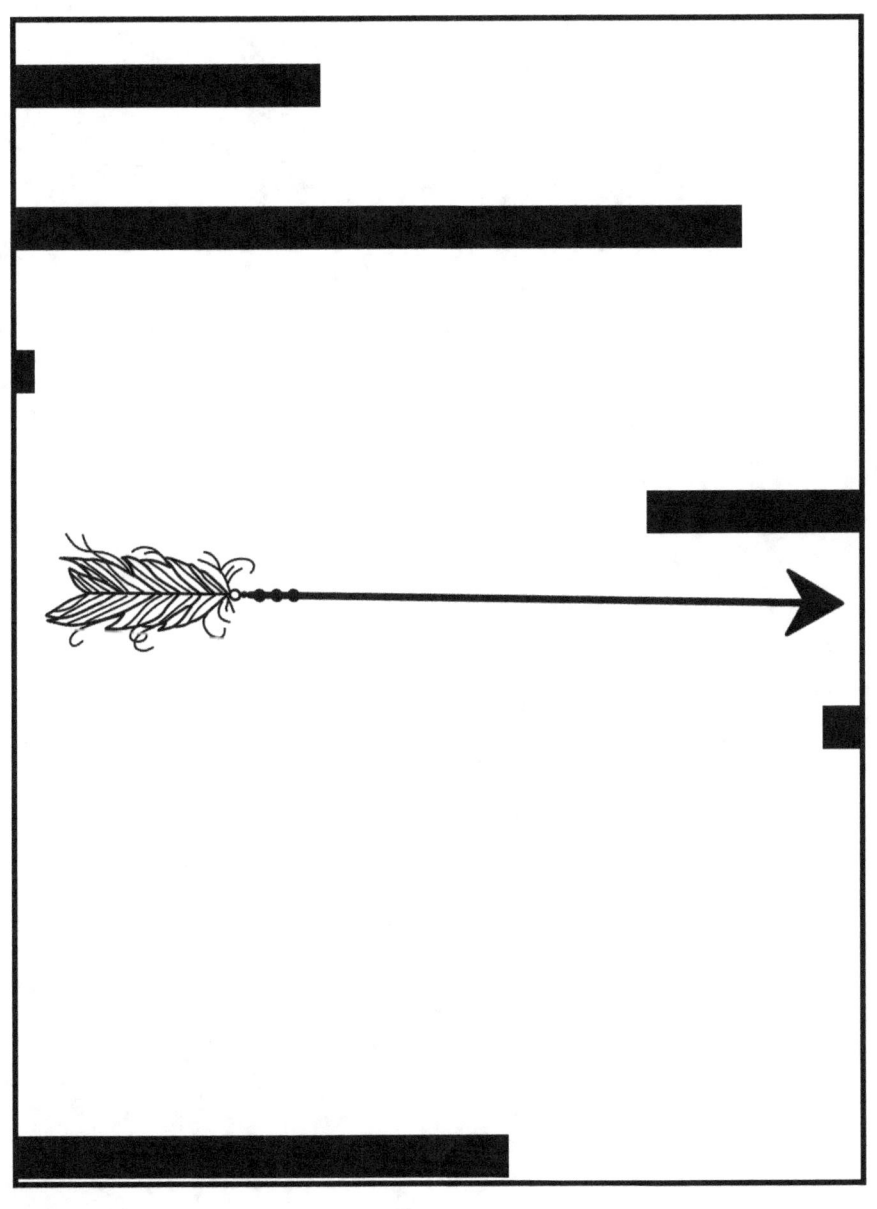

Chapter Sixteen

Servant Leadership

It is time for you to take everything you've learned and apply it as you step out in faith, taking your spot as a servant leader. This is what you have been praying for and dreaming of for so long. Now is your time. If you are still hesitant to begin and don't quite feel ready yet, I want to challenge you to learn more about your area of expertise. I still learn and grow not only around my field of expertise, but also in the areas that are personal to me, to ensure I am current with the trends and can lead and teach in a transforming world.

Influential leaders have the willingness to grow and develop with time. While some methods we learned previously are great foundational blocks for us to stand upon, they may not serve to assist those who God brings to us today. Take everything you know in your area of expertise and combine it to create your own unique methods, using scripture as your solid foundation. Build your methods in a way that strengthens your efforts as you serve others.

You can apply your growth anywhere; starting a business, writing a book, or volunteering for a charity. The key is to keep up with it and find new ways to make what you are doing interesting, exciting, and even challenging—so it keeps your interest for a longer time. Often, we give up because we lose interest in what we are doing. When you commit to growing and learning, you keep interest and intentionality at the forefront. You have almost all you need to get started.

A Second Chance

It's the first day back in my office after my time off from surgery, and I am attempting to work a partial day to see how my hand and arm function. Nervousness fills me as I wonder how long I can physically withstand the demands of moving the mouse. Music fills my office with songs of praise. I close my eyes and offer a prayer before I get started. I never again want to start a day of work without first asking God to lead me where He wants me to go.

In my time off after surgery, I put in many hours in prayer seeking direction on how to transition from graphic designer to servant leader focused on ministry. By now, I have come to terms with the idea that designing will look vastly different for me from here forward. God has revealed to me that I haven't completely lost the ability to design—but I also realize I am limited in how much I can do.

In my career, I became extremely prideful in how I design and the techniques I have worked hard to perfect. To keep my client roster full, I kept my techniques under wraps to ensure I was the one getting the bookings. What I realized, however, was that by gatekeeping how to learn a valuable skill, I am stopping others from advancing forward in their business.

It never occurred to me that perhaps I could teach others how to strengthen their skills in areas they were struggling. Not just in design, but also in business or authorship. I had allowed my tunnel vision to keep my focus solely on one skillset I possessed instead of realizing my fullest potential as a leader with many different skills and experiences.

One of the most beautiful things about time is that as it goes by, new generations rise and shine. As we age, we can either be a helping hand to assist the newer generations—or we can be stubborn and let our unique ways of doing things die with us. If all I have ever wanted to do was build a legacy I could be proud of and could leave behind when I pass from this earth, why am I not teaching everything I learned and know? It is up to us to lead new generations by being the example they need.

Throughout my life, I have had the privilege and honor of working for many businesses that range from small to large corporations. The skills I have learned along the way have helped me build an extremely successful business, and I know they will help others do the same. As I transition to becoming a creative director for other businesses, the idea of teaching younger designers lights that fire within. I know in doing so, I will have played a part in helping a newer generation of designers come to love design as much as I do, ensuring human creativity never dies off.

However, I feel we have reached an era where more advanced tools and shortcuts have taken out critical and creative thinking from us. Time is a valuable commodity and so is money, which is why these tools and shortcuts have become so popular. The word of caution I would give is to ensure you are not replacing your creative thinking with something that separates you from tapping into your time with God or diminishing the gifts He's given you. Creativity is a gift from God. We honor that precious gift by using our creativity in our own lives and to bless others.

The same applies to any of your other gifts. Use your God-given gifts often and share them with others. By obediently using your gifts in a way that pleases God, it becomes second nature as you grow and enhance your skills and talents in ways you've never thought possible.

In my disobedience, I ignored the clear direction to share my knowledge, fearing it would make me obsolete. God has graciously given me a second chance to try again—and I feel extreme gratitude as I work on making that a priority. It took setting my pride aside as I humbly stepped forward to serve others.

Your Own Thing

As I have drafted up a new business plan to transition to becoming a servant leader, old habits resurfaced; doubt began to cloud my judgment. The constant need to people-please was still a hurdle I had yet to clear. Letting go of things I had started at the request of friends or family made it feel impossible to avoid hurting feelings. Yet, I knew to scale my business and prepare for servant leadership, it had to be done.

Determined to wipe the slate clean and start over, I treated my business transition as I would coach a new client. I assigned myself a task to complete the workbooks I had created for my branding coaching. The discoveries revealed what was in my heart surrounding what I wanted for my business. My discoveries didn't surprise me, as I had already sensed a shift within myself.

Lessons in the effect of chronic people pleasing surfaced as I saw the consequences of my choices. Learning to differentiate between serving others and pleasing others has been a tough lesson.

When you serve others, you put their needs ahead of yours to help them get through whatever it is they face. When you please others, you put their needs ahead of yours to satisfy a want they have—sometimes at your expense.

To become a servant leader in the way you feel called, it is important to remember to trust that God will reveal to you what it is He wants you to do. Begin to trust your judgment as you make plans to do your own God-given thing without influence from others. If you struggle to discern how to set up a plan of action, find a Christian coach or mentor who specializes in what you are trying to achieve. Do you feel called to write a book? Seek a book coach who is in alignment with your goals. If God has told you to start a business, find a Christian business coach. Called to ministry? Search for a ministry coach or mentor.

By working with someone who knows and understands what you are struggling to do, you are allowing them the chance to use their God-given gifts to serve you—all while experiencing growth along the way. Collaborating with other Christian creatives has helped me break through so many of my barriers. I fully believe God has brought exactly who I needed at the time I needed them.

Where I'm Going

Throughout this book, I have shared with you the evolution of my business. But I have yet to disclose where I am going now. In my workbook process, I uncovered the answer to a question I have been asking myself for years—who is my ideal client? I've wrestled with determining if my ideal client is an entrepreneur, a leader in an organization, a writer, or a creative. The answer that came to me during discovery was that my client is likely more than simply one of these things—making her a multi-passionate woman with many different ideas and interests.

My business lineup has always felt choppy and separated into different offerings that felt disconnected from each other. I had a goal to simplify by combining everything cohesively and restructuring the offerings to better assist my ideal client. In chapter thirteen, I shared with you about my newest project, *Boldly Woven Magazine*. This new project is the beginning of a movement I am creating to better serve multi-passionate women with plans to add more in-person experiences to deepen their faith while also learning new skills.

Within my business, I have combined everything I learned from my stationery brand, subscription box, graphic design services, coaching, writing, podcasts, and all experiences into core offerings that make more sense for my client. Leading with a teaching-first approach, I am now available for consulting and coaching to help others learn the skills needed to achieve their goals.

Continuing with my core value of collaboration, I am also creating opportunities for others to join forces with me to share their gifts in new ways. My business has fully become my ministry, and the way I will honor God for all He has done for me by helping others.

So many women want to do everything themselves, yet often lack the knowledge to get where they hope to be. If I can be a small part in helping teach them the skills they need and instilling confidence in them, then I have begun to fulfill what I am being called to do.

There is still one enormous piece to the puzzle in fulfilling my calling in its entirety—and that, my friend, is a work in progress. The exciting part is that it is now possible to achieve my goal because I have a clear direction and have put my plan in place.

The Unseen Truth

I had to put pride aside and wipe the slate clean to begin my transition into becoming a servant leader. In my discovery process, I learned the valuable lesson of differentiating between serving people and pleasing people. Ultimately, this has led me to the destination God had in mind for me. I can take everything He has given me over the years and combine all the knowledge to create a ministry that honors Him.

Think back over your lifetime. Make a list of all the skills, techniques, and experiences you have had. Spend time in prayer while reflecting on your list, asking God to reveal the direction you need to take now. Give Him thanks for revealing to you all He has done to equip you throughout your lifetime to prepare you in becoming a servant leader now. Your list is proof that you are ready.

How do you feel rediscovering your gifts and areas of expertise? Do you see a clearer defined path towards a life serving others for God? If you struggle to make the connection, go backwards a step. Keep discovering those skills, techniques, and experiences you've had throughout your lifetime. There may be something you've forgotten. Be sure to write everything, even if it is small.

What is it I am feeling called to do now?

Braver with Belief

> *"Am I now trying to win the approval of human beings, or of God? Or am I trying to please people? If I were still trying to please people, I would not be a servant of Christ."*
> Galatians 1:10

In order to become braver with belief, we have to learn the hard lesson of differentiating between pleasing people and serving people. Spend time in prayer seeking God's instruction before saying yes as you decide to help someone. If you have a bad feeling in the pit of your stomach, this may be a good indicator that it is okay to say no. Don't feel obligated to always say yes to helping others. God will help guide you in the direction you should go when you take time to invite Him into the conversation.

As you step into the role of servant leader, it is important to always have a God-first approach. You are doing this for His approval only—not that of others. Maintaining this approach can be difficult when we seek validation or recognition for our actions. Whatever you do, do it with a humble heart, without expectation.

Are you able to share everything you know without getting credit for the work being done by the person you taught? This dying of self is a humble lesson on its own. Teaching others means leaving them with the knowledge and skill to do something you know how to do. Their work is theirs alone to receive credit. Rest in the assurance that God is proud of you for the part you played in helping them honor Him, too.

The Strength in Letting Go

We can learn so much from the actions of Jesus. In John Chapter 13, we read the story of Jesus washing the feet of his disciples. While this may not seem relevant today, when you consider the state of the world during that time frame, it changes the perspective. The disciples walked everywhere, while wearing sandals. Imagine dirt-covered feet. Would you want to touch them? Now, picture Jesus, the King of Kings, humbly kneeling before the disciples with a bowl of water, as He lovingly washes their feet in an example of what it means to lead in love.

What we see in this example is someone who put themselves last to show the power of serving others. He didn't have to wash their dirty, tired feet. He wanted to do it. When we serve others, it is important that we put ourselves last, allowing them the chance to be transformed by God. God will work in and through you as you do this.

It's time to let go of the need to be first—to become last as you serve others. By loving others as they are, you are showing them that their lives matter. People today are hurting and suffering. They feel as if they don't belong, and some even question their existence. By stepping into a servant leader role, you are the light in their darkness. Lead them to Jesus.

Moving Forward with Hope

Being a servant leader in your business, ministry, or personal life means you are actively choosing to put the needs of others before your own. In our desire to be more like Jesus, may we always remember His instruction to do as He has done.

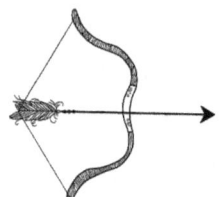

Move forward with confidence, knowing you are now the one to instill hope in the lives of countless others as you honor God by fulfilling your calling.

Braver Choices

Actionable steps you can take to become braver with belief as you step into the role of servant leader. I have broken it down for you in a way that is easier to remember: B.R.A.V.E.R.

Brighten: An action taking call to service to refine our hearts as we discover the area in which to serve.

Serve Others: Volunteer to mentor someone in an area you are an expert. Share your wisdom and gifts with them, helping them in any way you can.

Reflect: A prayer that covers the emotions felt within each chapter with a promise to let go of the things we need to, so we can keep moving forward.

> *Father, I am so sorry for pleasing people instead of pleasing you. Help me let go of the need to be first and help me become last as I serve others. Please forgive me for not seeking You first, as I planned out my*

transition to becoming a servant leader. I hope to be a shining light so others may find you. Amen.

Act: An action taking exercise that forces us to get up and move forward.

Journal Prompt: The importance of servant leadership in my personal and professional life is...

Verse: Memorization of a Bible verse that helps us remember the lesson within the chapter.

Write the following scripture and post it somewhere you'll see it every day; a bathroom mirror, refrigerator, or your home office. Memorize it and refer to it for a reminder to serve like Jesus.

> *"Now that I, your Lord and Teacher, have washed your feet, you also should wash one another's feet. I have set you an example that you should do as I have done for you."*
> John 13:14-15

Explore: An action taking exercise to help us explore new possibilities we may not have yet thought of.

Exercise: Goals as a Servant Leader - write your goals in becoming a servant leader. Be very specific and set dates you'd like to achieve the goals.

Renew: A journal prompt for us to reflect with God in solitude.

Journal Prompt: What God has revealed to me by reading Braver with Belief...

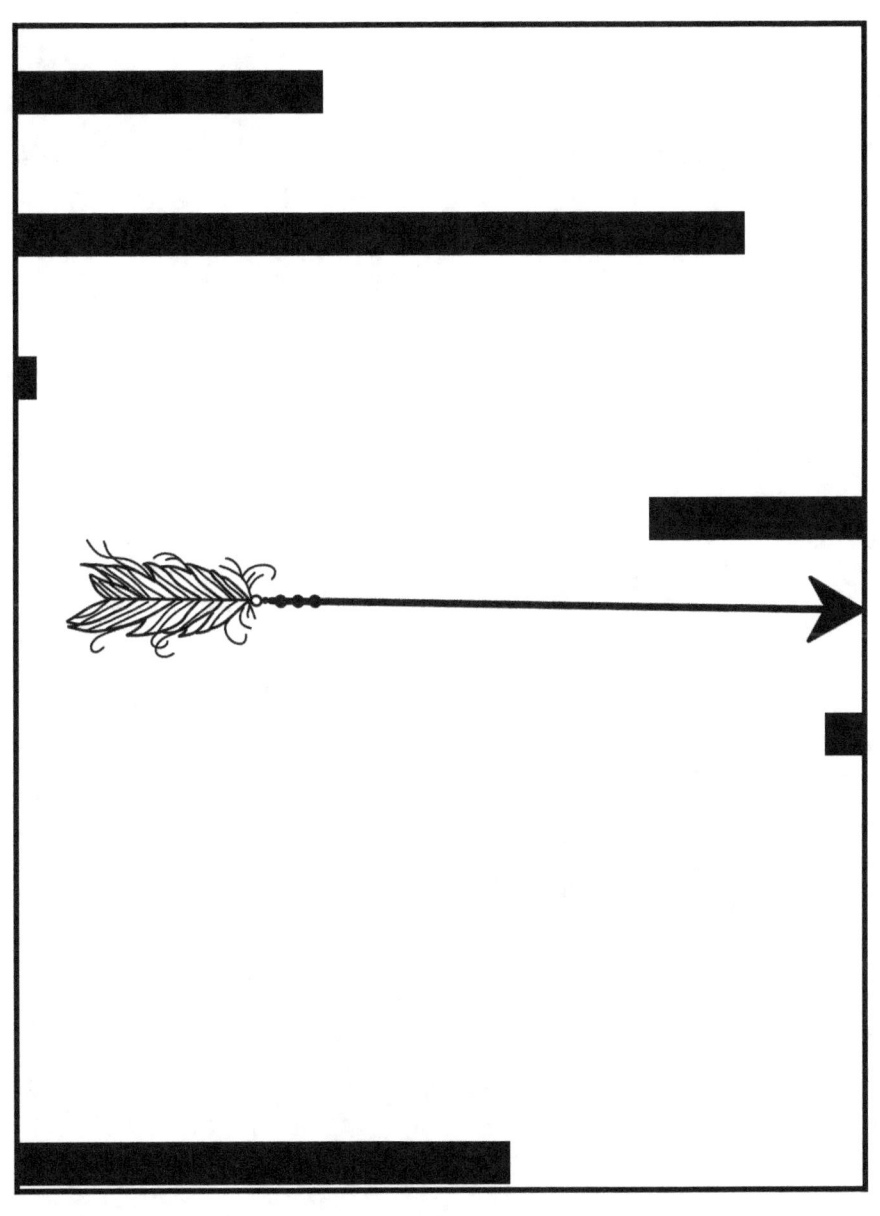

Acknowledgements

So Very Grateful

I can never find the words to properly express the level of gratitude I have for those who have gone out of their way to make a difference in my life, but I'm going to try my best.

First and foremost, I want to express gratitude to Mike, my steadfast supporter of all that I ever hope for and dream of.

As my husband, you see all the parts of me that not everyone else sees, including the downright messy ones. Your unwavering love through every storm we've weathered together has been the sunshine through the dark clouds. I am thankful for the helping hands you've lent, not just over the years, but also when I literally couldn't use my own. Everything you've done has helped me in so many ways. I truly hope you know how much I love and appreciate you for all you do. Thank you for being a sounding board when I need to talk through the jumble of thoughts and for helping me remember how great things are for us, even through the trials. You reminded me I have what it takes to be a leader when I doubted and shared valuable resources to help me learn more. I cannot imagine my life without you in it. Growing old with you will forever and always be my greatest blessing and honor. I love you, always and forever.

To my children, even still now, you are teaching me valuable life lessons through memories that pop up now and then. It was an absolute honor serving as your foster mom for two years. Though visually the signs of your presence have faded, the permanence of you will forever remain in my heart. It is a joy seeing where life takes you into adulthood and I continually pray for you.

To my Family, through all the difficulties life has thrown us, you've never wavered in your presence in my life. We often get caught up in living our own lives with physical distance separating us. Nevertheless, I live for the moments we get to gather and celebrate all the goodness life has for us. Thank you for helping me make every single moment count. I am who I am because of your significant influence. I'm so grateful for you, Mom and Dad, for keeping a watchful eye over Mike and me, not only during the inclement weather, but also for our wellbeing. Just knowing you are looking out for our safety brings warmth and joy to have you both in our lives.

To my extended Family, thank you for your encouragement over the years to never give up, and for loving me for who I am. You mean so much to me.

To Mike's Family, thank you for your support, encouragement, and all the incredible memories we've made over the years. You each hold a special place in my heart.

To Jamie, thank you for the incredible life-changing gift to see P!nk in concert. You made the evening more than memorable, and I will always remember the feeling of belonging that accompanied it. What an amazing opportunity to cross off something from my bucket list with you. I live for our Monday evening video calls and am so grateful for your friendship. You have inspired me in so many ways over the years just by being the incredible woman you are. Thank you for challenging me to be the best possible version of myself that I can be. A million thank you's don't feel like enough.

To Tracy, my football mom club friend, brought to me because of my children. You are one of my favorite gifts they gave me. I am forever grateful for you in so many ways. You have played an integral part in me becoming the healthiest version of myself by helping me navigate the medical field in our area. When I was literally knocked down this year, you stepped in and helped me out, no questions asked. Thank you for always checking in on me and reminding me that God is still present with me, even when I face trials. Those reminders pushed me to finish this book after wanting to give up on it.

To Carrie, thank you for gently pushing me back out there. You saw I was ready before I did, and intuitively nudged me right when I needed it most. That gentle push reignited the spark needed to remember my calling and has continued to grow since. I am so grateful for all the things you do (which we both know is a ton) to help me out when I need it. You have been pivotal in helping me make the preparations for *Boldly Woven* and what awaits the biggest movement I've ever created. Thank you for sharing your heart and talents with me.

To Megan, you patiently waited for me to come back to a place where I could be more present as a friend. Thank you for waiting for me, and for coming to support me at events. I am so grateful for your friendship. You make me laugh, sometimes really hard, on days when I am down. Your ideas and encouragement surrounding *Boldly Woven* have played a large part in helping me with clarity and direction needed to make it happen. Thank you for never skipping a beat, and always being a faithful friend.

To Amanda, thank you for keeping me accountable by checking in with daily devotions. I look forward to each morning as we learn and grow in Christ, together. I'm so grateful we agreed to do these devotions daily, many years ago. It has been an opportunity to deepen my faith while also strengthening our relationship. Thank you for always checking in and lifting me up when I need it most. I'm so grateful for the amazing friend you are.

To my amazing friend group, each of you have been absolutely amazing not just to each other, but to me as well. I'm so grateful for the bonds we've shared over the years and the friendships that have grown and flourished. Thank you for showering me with love during recovery from surgery.

To all my friends, life would be *oh so lonely* without you in it. So many of you have played a major part in my life. And while I wish I could shout you all out, please know you are on my heart right now as I am typing this. Thank you for loving me unconditionally, as my most authentic self.

To Tami, thank you for your willingness to coach me while I was going through my season of healing. You had the toughest job and the strongest shoulders. I'm so grateful for your compassion as you allowed me to speak freely about what was on my heart, even the downright messy stuff. The incredible gifts you have to help make sense of all those jumbled up thoughts is a breath of fresh air. Thank you for the big shifts you've helped me make as together, we knocked down barriers to help me keep moving forward. Thank you for all the prayers and shared scriptures to keep me anchored in Christ. I thank God for you daily.

To Niki, I am so grateful for the chance to work with you on this book. You were the person I prayed God would bring to help me take it to new heights while guarding my voice and perspective. Working with you has been an absolute joy. You lovingly pushed me to dig deeper and share more vulnerability in each chapter to help make this book more relatable with my readers. Your love for God shines through all you do. Thank you for all your hard work editing this book. I look forward to not only working with you on other projects, but also seeing where our new friendship takes us.

To my clients, thank you for your grace and understanding during my season of healing. You patiently awaited my return to work and filled up my calendar post-surgery. Though designing looks differently for me now, your understanding of longer turn around times has been humbling. I'm *oh so honored* you continue to choose me to serve you.

To Ashley, my Dietician at Clearcreek Nutrition & Wellness Co, you single-handedly changed my life. When we first spoke, I was skeptical of the impact your program would have on me and my overall wellbeing, but there was something in the way you connected with me by meeting me right where I was. I doubted if I could make such a big lifestyle change and maintain it. But with your help, I have proven the impossible is possible. You have freed me in so many ways, mostly in removing my limiting beliefs surrounding food. Thank you for the hard work you've put into helping me solve my complex case and pinpointing the cause of my many issues. Life is so much more enjoyable now that I feel better to enjoy it, and I owe that to you. God brought me to you because He knew I needed the best in the industry to get me the help I needed.

To my Physical Therapists at Southview Therapy at Yankee, you had your work cut out for you when you got me as your patient. I arrived to you frightened, frustrated, and angry. I'm so grateful for Tyler, who patiently worked with me on regaining the use of my right hand and arm after surgery. Your compassion coupled with professionalism showed me that there are still incredible workers in the medical field who care about their patients. Thank you for taking the time to explain things to me so I could understand, and for celebrating every single win each week, even if it was small. I fully believe God placed me in your care to ensure I could get to where I am now because of your help.

To all the Future servant leaders, thank you for taking the time to read my book. I pray the lessons were valuable insight to you as you determine the direction of your calling. Rest in the assurance that you have what it takes to be a great leader. May God keep watch over you as you boldly lead for Him. I'm so proud of you for answering your call.

And to Jesus, thank you for sharing that sacred dance with me and reminding me how much you love me. When I am broken, you safely hold me closer to you as you give me the space needed to let it all out. I'm so grateful for the life you gave so that I may live mine. Thank you for choosing me to serve you, I am honored to be your servant leader.

About the Author

Shonda Ramsey is a friend, encourager, and leader. She is passionate about helping others feel loved, wanted, and understood. Shonda is a multi-passionate entrepreneur and author. After overcoming personal struggles and discovering a passion for helping women walk in their God-given identity, she authored her first book, *Authentically Anchored*. With a love of writing dating back to her childhood, Shonda has always found comfort and strength in her words, from speech contests to church devotions.

In addition to writing, Shonda offers graphic design services for authors and entrepreneurs, specializing in book covers, branding, and book formatting. She hosted the podcast *Dear Indie Author*, where she shared insights and support for fellow writers navigating the world of independent publishing. Taking what she learned from the podcast, Shonda has transitioned the concept behind the podcast to a column in her ministry through *Boldly Woven Magazine*. Her experience through personal hardships has fueled her mission to connect with women, offering them a place to share their stories of hope and resilience.

Shonda lives in Ohio with her husband, Mike, and their Yorkie, Coco. In her free time, she enjoys camping with her husband, laughing with friends, singing, and dancing in the rain. Her goal is to write books that resonate deeply with her readers by covering real and challenging topics while ending on a positive and hopeful note through a deepening of faith. Through her writing and design work, she aims to inspire faith, authenticity, strength, and the courage to be one's true self.

If Shonda can be of service to you as you move forward, she would love to connect with you at www.shondaramsey.com.

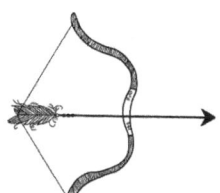

This new beginning you face is the start of a revival.

You are called to serve.